Henry Cooper

Cut Eyes
&
Left Hooks

Jim Kirkwood

Dalcumly Press

First published in the UK in 2016

Dalcumly Press
10 Forest Grove
Kilmarnock, Ayrshire KA3 1UP

Copyright © Jim Kirkwood 2016

All rights reserved. This book is sold subject to the condition that it shall not by way of trade or otherwise be lent, resold, reproduced, hired out or otherwise circulated without the publisher's prior consent in writing.

ISBN 978-0-9569253-3-6

Papers used in this book are natural, renewable and recyclable products sourced from well-managed forests.

Typeset in Adobe Garamond, designed and produced by Gilmour Print, www.self-publish-books.co.uk

Contents

	Acknowledgments	*iv*
	Introduction	*v*
Chapter 1:	An Early Loss to Joe Erskine	1
Chapter 2:	Four Defeats in a Row	8
Chapter 3:	Cooper Crashes the World's Top Five	16
Chapter 4:	British and Empire Champion	23
Chapter 5:	Erskine Defeated at Last	32
Chapter 6:	First Lonsdale Belt, but Disaster Follows	38
Chapter 7:	Cooper Dominates British Heavyweight Scene	44
Chapter 8:	The Famous Left Hook	50
Chapter 9:	A Second Lonsdale Belt	58
Chapter 10:	Successful Year Ends in Failure	64
Chapter 11:	The World Title Fight	70
Chapter 12:	Knocked Out by Patterson, but Third Lonsdale Belt Secured	78
	Photograph Section between pages 88 and 89	
Chapter 13:	The Fight that Never Happened	89
Chapter 14:	Unforgettable Ending	98
	Conclusion	*113*
	Fight Record	*117*

Acknowledgements

Henry Cooper: An Autobiography (1972)
Henry Cooper by Robert Edwards (2002)
A Hero For All Time by Norman Giller (2012)
Boxing News 1954-1971
Various national newspapers
Various recordings by the BBC
Derek Rowe, photographer,
George Zeleny, boxing historian
Chas Taylor, boxing historian
Be Lucky by Andrew Sumner (2008)
Box On by Harry Gibbs (1981)
When The Gloves Come Off by Billy Walker (2007)
Chuvalo: A Fighter's Life by George Chuvalo (2013)
Muhammad Ali by Thomas Hauser (1991)
King Henry – The fighting life of Henry Cooper by Peter Wilson
www.boxrec.com
www.youtube.com

Introduction

WHY WOULD ANYONE FEEL THE NEED TO WRITE YET ANOTHER BIOGRAPHY / autobiography on Sir Henry Cooper? There have been at least three excellent attempts already – *Henry Cooper: An Autobiography*, compiled by John Samuels (1972), *Henry Cooper* by Robert Edwards (2002) and *A Hero For All Time* by Norman Giller (2012). The first was a painstakingly detailed life story, the second was a much needed update, and the last was a valuable insight by a journalistic friend who had access to the Cooper 'inner circle'. I have read and enjoyed them all and would advise anyone who hasn't done so to acquire them.

There are two reasons why I've written this book. The first is purely selfish. Sir Henry Cooper was one of my childhood heroes. When I was still at primary school I used to say to my dad that when I grew up I wanted to be 6' 1" tall and weigh 13st. When he asked why I would tell him that this was Henry Cooper's measurements (in actual fact Cooper was slightly taller and heavier!). I remember also having the occasional nightmares when suffering from the usual childhood illnesses. For some obscure reason my mother would find me mumbling 'Cassius Clay' or even 'Stanley Matthews'. Why a young boy from Ayrshire in Scotland who supported Glasgow Rangers and worshipped Jim Baxter and Denis Law should be concerned about Stanley Matthews defies explanation. However, the fact I was having nightmares about Cassius Clay was capable of some understanding due to his defeat of my hero in 1963 and the blood flowing freely from Sir Henry's cut eye.

So, researching and putting together this book has been an absolute pleasure, a 'labour of love' if you will. Part of the enjoyment has been the discovery of facts and situations which I hadn't known about at the time, or had forgotten and glossed over. Which brings me to the second reason for writing the book, and possibly more relevant to the reader.

I hope the authors of the three books I've mentioned will forgive me for my comments, they are certainly not meant to be criticisms, but they were written from a 'Cooper perspective'. In other words they were written from the 'inside looking out' as opposed to the opposite point of view. They were based on interviews with Sir Henry and his opinions, memories and beliefs on his career, but the nature of the books were such that they didn't take account of how his fights and performances fitted into the heavyweight boxing picture in Britain, Europe and the rest of the world.

When journalists are writing their columns for newspapers and magazines they don't know what the future holds. What this allows the researcher to do is to take the facts at the time from these articles and assess the situation with the benefit of hindsight. Of course much of this is speculation and as such can be treated with a degree of caution. Nevertheless, it does provide an independent view, hopefully free from bias and favouritism.

I believe it's important to Sir Henry's memory to put his boxing career into context. We need to know how his career progressed and to do that properly we require to examine what was happening around him in the boxing world. There were critical moments when he could quite easily have made the decision to 'walk away' and it's likely he'd now simply be a distant memory for those hardcore, dyed in the wool, boxing fans. Fortunately for us those 'critical' moments passed and the rest, as they say, is now history.

There was a fear when I started out on this project that I'd discover that Sir Henry was a pretty average boxer, and nothing much more than a 'media creation'. Thankfully this never happened. He was not a myth. I hope you find the book interesting and consider my views fair. If I've succeeded, your opinion of Sir Henry may be enhanced, and if that's the case, I'd be delighted.

(You will note that the title of the book and all mention of the subject from here on will refer to him as either 'Cooper' or 'Henry', and not Sir Henry. Please forgive me, the reason is that the book covers the period before he was knighted).

CHAPTER ONE

An Early Loss to Joe Erskine

IN 1954, WHEN ROCKY MARCIANO WAS WORLD CHAMPION AND BRITAIN'S boxing press believed our own Don Cockell may yet provide a suitable challenger, the next generation of heavyweight hopefuls were emerging. Joe Erskine, Dick Richardson, Brian London, Henry Cooper and possibly Peter Bates formed the group and depending on your preference either man could rise to the top. London based bookmakers at the time produced odds on who would reach the British title first, with Erskine being the favourite, with Brian London, Cooper and Richardson just behind.

Erskine, London and Cooper had been ABA champions, usually a strong indication their professional careers could follow suit, but Welshman Richardson was a giant of a man for that generation and Peter Bates, whose career in the paid ranks had started earlier, were creating some interest due to their winning runs. Although Cooper's career had begun in a blaze of publicity, when he signed his pro contract live on TV, he was by no means considered a great star in the making. But the potential was there, of that there was no doubt.

Cooper's first five fights all ended inside the distance and it wasn't until February 1955 he would reach the end of a fight and hear the referee's scorecard being read out, when he beat Cliff Purnell at Harringay Arena. By this time the Somerset based Purnell had taken part in twenty five fights, losing only four inside the allotted distance. Two months previously he'd lost on points to both Erskine and Bates, and it might have been thought, as Cooper couldn't improve on the efforts of both, by stopping Purnell, that he wasn't progressing any quicker than his contemporaries.

Cooper's next big test was two months, and three fights, later. This time he was put in with the tough Jamaican, Joe Bygraves. Now based in Liverpool, Bygraves was a very experienced operator having won twenty four of twenty nine contests, including a victory over Peter Bates. It was going to be a real test for the young

Cooper, and it was certainly a significant step up in class. Having only had his first professional fight some seven months previously it was the type of contest which would never be considered in the modern day game.

Bygraves was a real 'character'. He turned professional just before the amateur code banned him for life after he knocked out a referee in the dressing room after he'd disqualified him earlier in the night! During the fight with Cooper, Bygraves tired badly and Henry almost had him out in the last round, but had to settle for another points victory.

Eight days later Henry experienced his first loss, in his first fight as a professional against a foreign boxer. When his opponent, Uber Bacilieri, arrived in London it was the Italian's fourth visit to these shores. Bacilieri was slightly shorter than Cooper but ten pounds heavier. He'd already won and lost his national title, and just over three weeks earlier had taken future world champion, Ingemar Johansson, to a points verdict. No mean feat when you consider the power of the Swede, as would be ably demonstrated against Henry himself two years later. That being said, on his previous visits to Britain he'd lost to Don Cockell and Jack Gardner, but beaten the lightly regarded Polly Smith.

Cooper started well enough being able to land with ease on his more experienced foe and he came back to his corner at the end of the first round well contented with his work. That all changed in the next round when after an exchange of blows the referee stepped in and saw a two inch cut over Henry's right eye. Cooper always claimed the cut came from a clash of heads and manager Jim Wicks threw in the towel when he saw the damage.

A defeat, especially due to a cut eye, was not a career threatening event in those days. Modern day professionals are primarily 'ticket sellers' with promoters depending on them to offload sufficient briefs to family and friends to finance the fight. An unbeaten record becomes ultra important as it encourages the casual fan to believe they're watching a future champion. Boxing had a wider and better informed fan base in the 1950s, the paying public going along to boxing promotions to be entertained and to evaluate the capabilities of the fighters. Already, those attending the Jack Solomons shows, knew that Cooper had the skills and the punch to be a real threat in the heavyweight division and a cut eye defeat to a former Italian champion was neither here nor there.

Henry Cooper: Cut Eyes and Left Hooks

From the same show at Harringay it became clear that Solomons was building up interest in the rising heavyweight stars and stoking up the competition to find out who would ultimately come out on top. The only one missing from the 'famous five' was Brian London who'd just completed the demolition of his first two opponents. Erskine was clearly the front runner. He won again in this his twentieth fight, all victories except for an early draw. Richardson too kept his run going – eight wins from ten and seven inside the distance. Bates had the same number of fights as Erskine with eleven of his sixteen wins by KO. Crucially though he'd lost to both Erskine and Bygraves.

From examination of their respective records at the time the big punchers were Cooper, Richardson and Bates, with Erskine being acknowledged as a superb boxer but without the 'dig' to go with it. As far as Solomons and the rest of the British boxing public were concerned these were the heavyweights who would go forward in the hope that at least one of them would emulate Don Cockell with regard to his challenge for Marciano's world title.

Cooper recovered reasonably quickly from his cut eye to stop Ron Harman in June at Nottingham and after the summer recess Jim Wicks wisely matched him with Bacilieri again at the White City on 13 September. Once more Solomons had all the prospects on the same bill, excluding London, and speculation was rife that there would soon be a match-up between them to decide who was going to proceed as the leader. The first stage in this process was the pairing of Richardson with Bates while Erskine was scheduled to take on previous Cooper victim, Harman. A few weeks before the event Erskine had outpointed Bacilieri and of course the pundits were going to draw comparisons. It was speculated that the winner of the Richardson v Bates clash would take on either Erskine or Cooper with that particular contest already being planned.

Jim Wicks would later suggest that Henry knew he had the beating of Bacilieri and was looking to get a few rounds under his belt against continental opposition. As it turned out the Italian was knocked cold by a left hook in the seventh round. When Harman pulled out Erskine ended up fighting another Italian and surprisingly, for him, won inside the distance. Most impressive however was Richardson who knocked out Bates in the third round. A good night's work for all concerned, except for poor Peter Bates, with Solomons scheme gaining momentum.

Jim Kirkwood

Since the time Henry had turned pro he'd been training most evenings at the Thomas a' Becket pub on the Old Kent Road. His former amateur coach, Georgie Page, had came along with him and worked beside Danny Holland. Page was a 'true blue' amateur and wanted to have his own gym where he and Henry could train alone. Training at the Thomas a' Becket meant mixing with other boxers and trainers. It's easy to perceive that Page would have begun to get annoyed with the interference and there must surely have been conflict between him and Danny Holland. Holland was Wicks's 'man', and it must have seemed to Page that the 'writing was on the wall'. Around the time of the Bacilieri fight Page decided to 'up sticks' and leave. Being the type of character he was, and his closeness to Cooper, the move must have upset Henry, but by now he'd built up a trust with Wicks and relied completely on his decision making, so the 'train chugged along' relatively undisturbed.

In October, Erskine, unusually, had another inside the distance victory back in his native soil at Cardiff and Richardson too had a couple of early wins. But the big one was lined up by Solomons, and it was accepted as an eliminator for the British title. Cooper would face Erskine at Harringay on 15 November.

Cooper and Erskine were friends due to having done their National Service together in the same regiment. Henry had beaten Joe in the semi final of the light heavyweight ABAs three years previously, but as the fight approached the boxing public were generally predicting a victory for the Welshman. They would eventually go on to fight each other five times in the professional game and Cooper always had great respect for his opponent. He was a very skilful boxer and Henry genuinely felt that if he'd had the punch to match his technical ability he might well have ended up a serious challenger for the world title.

On the night, the bout went the full ten round distance and much to the disappointment of the Cooper team, Erskine took the decision. Cooper hurt his hand in the seventh round punching the top of Erskine's head but had to admit the Welshman was perhaps just a bit too clever for him on the night. Although the result made it a bad night for Cooper, it could have ended a lot worse because he was involved in a serious road accident while driving home with his brothers George and Bernard, and Bernard's pregnant wife.

Cockell was still the British champion but hadn't defended it for over two years due to his attempt to secure the world title fight with Marciano. Even after his annihilation, he continued fighting, and losing, to foreign opposition. Solomons was still eyeing a match between Erskine and Richardson but the British Boxing Board intervened and instructed there should be a final eliminator between Erskine and yet another Welshman, Johnny Williams.

Solomons then began planning a Cooper v Richardson contest, but this did not stop all those involved continuing to fight other opponents. In mid January Erskine beat foreign opposition in Cardiff and was booed out of the ring due primarily to his inability to put his Belgian opponent away. The following night in London, on a Stan Baker promotion, Richardson stopped another visitor, but more pertinently to Henry, and with unfortunate consequences for the victor, in the longer term, Brian London totally destroyed Cooper's brother George (or Jim as he was known professionally). George had been handily outpointing the clumsy London for the first three rounds before being smashed to the canvas repeatedly prior to being saved by the referee in the fourth.

It was well known in boxing circles that Henry and his twin were very close. They trained together, sparred together and were invariably in each other's corner during fights. On several occasions in the future Henry would take on opponents who'd beaten George, and publicly admitted several times when interviewed, often years later, that when he entered the ring for those fights he was seeking revenge on behalf of his brother. This might not seem remarkable but Cooper was normally a mild mannered individual who usually looked upon boxing as simply a business, having no particular dislike for whoever he was facing. London would be a notable exception.

Cooper was out of the ring for over three months returning in February at the Royal Albert Hall against French champion Maurice Mols. The visitor had won less than half of his twenty three contests, one of those defeats coming at the hands of Bacilieri, in Italy. Henry punished Mols forcing the referee to intervene in the fourth round.

In February and March Erskine and Richardson fought again in Wales where they naturally attracted huge crowds. Richardson stopped Erskine's former Belgian opposition Limage, while Erskine outpointed the German, Nurnberg. These results were ideal preparation for a fight between the two winners of Solomon's unofficial competition the previous year, and as it would unfold, an eliminator for the soon to be vacated British title. With Jim Wicks seeing a number of routes being cut off, and determined to keep Cooper in contention, he went public and offered £1,000 to either Erskine, Richardson, Bates or London if they were prepared to take on Henry. At present day values that equates to £25,000.

On the scene came former world light heavyweight champion, Freddie Mills, who was dipping his feet into the promotional business. He presented purse offers of over £1,000 each to both London and Cooper's management teams. Although many felt this opportunity was coming too soon for London, the offer, plus the £1,000 side stake put up by Wicks was too much to refuse and the fight was scheduled for the Empress Hall at Earls Court on 1 May.

As the date of the contest approached London became the slight favourite probably due to his unbeaten record and the battering handed out to Henry's brother in January. In preparation for the fight Cooper was sparring the current champion Don Cockell but this probably would have been little help as Cockell was on a very steep slope downwards towards boxing oblivion. It should be recognised that Jim Wicks was not known as someone to risk his money unnecessarily. To have a side stake of such amount going to the winner, it's safe to assume Cooper's manager had little doubt about the outcome, and he was proved right.

A fired up Cooper came out in the first round and landed a solid right to the body. London brought his hands down briefly and was blasted into the ropes by a left hook. Henry pummelled away at the defenceless London until the referee had no option but to step in and stop it. Cooper later claimed that if he'd stopped punching and stepped back earlier London would have collapsed, implying that it was only the force of his punches which were keeping him up.

This was a very early example of the often hidden contrast between Cooper the man and Cooper the boxer. Outside the ring Henry was quite rightly known as a complete gentleman, a characteristic which in the future would endear him to the entire nation, but inside the ropes he could be totally ruthless and on occasion even going beyond what would be considered 'sporting' behaviour in those far off days when Britain was known for its sense of 'fair play'.

Six days after Cooper's resounding victory over London, 35,000 fans (yes, thirty five thousand) turned up at the Maindy Stadium in Cardiff to see Joe Erskine push himself right to the front of British heavyweight boxing when he superbly outpointed his much bigger and more aggressive compatriot, Dick Richardson. With Cockell still to officially surrender his British title, Erskine was, as we know, scheduled to fight Johnny Williams in a final eliminator, while simultaneously the Boxing News trade paper had elevated him to the number nine contender for the world title now vacant due to Marciano's retirement.

In June, Cooper fought for the first time as a professional at Wembley, on a Harry Levene promotion. His opponent was another Italian, Giannino Luise, while topping the bill was an Empire championship contest between Joe Bygraves and Kitione Lave. Henry's great form continued with the Italian unable to cope with Cooper's left hand work. Although cut again on the left eyebrow, Henry controlled the fight comfortably and was hurting Luise with left hooks to the body. The end came in the seventh round when another attack left the visitor helpless on the ropes, his arms dangling by his side.

As the summer break arrived two events occurred, both to Cooper's benefit. Firstly, Cockell finally retired allowing the British Boxing Board to raise the forthcoming Erskine v Williams match from eliminator to championship status. At the same time they indicated that the winner should face Cooper. Moreover, Wicks had struck a deal with a Manchester promoter to put on a show at Belle Vue in September featuring almost all the boxers in Wicks's stable including Henry. Cooper's opponent would be Peter Bates, who'd recovered from his loss to Richardson by travelling to Germany and beating the European light heavyweight champion.

At the end of August, Erskine clearly outpointed Johnny Williams and became the first of the new breed to win a title, and have the Lonsdale belt strapped round his waist. It'd been a bruising contest resulting in cut eyes for the new champion meaning a quick defence against Cooper looked unlikely. Nevertheless Henry needed to look impressive against Bates on 7 September to maintain the momentum.

CHAPTER 2

Four Defeats in a Row

IN 1956 EVERYONE SEEMED TO UNDERSTAND AND ACCEPT THE RULES GOVERNING world championship boxing even though they weren't written down. This was made easier because there were only eight weight divisions, and all the champions were universally recognised. The basic rule on how to become the champion was very clear. A boxer simply had to beat the current holder. However the status quo was beginning to be challenged probably due to the increasing amount of money involved through television coverage in America.

Three American organisations had great influence on who should fight the champions – the National Boxing Association, the New York State Athletic Commission and, incredibly, the Ring Magazine, edited by Nat Fleischer. The Ring would publish who they believed were the contenders in their regular ratings, and to be fair, before the introduction of modern day technology, they did a pretty reasonable job.

When Cooper was about to take on Peter Bates in September 1956 the winds of change were sweeping through world heavyweight boxing. The champion Rocky Marciano had retired undefeated, causing utter confusion. It'd been twenty eight years since this had happened before, when Gene Tunney gave up the crown, thus creating the opening for organised crime syndicates to take control. Nobody wanted this to happen again, but as underworld figures were already wielding great power, it seemed unavoidable.

Britain's two most powerful promoters were watching the situation closely and were making efforts to become more involved. Harry Levene was in communication with the NYSAC publicising that his new deal with Wembley Stadium could make it a future venue for a world heavyweight title fight. Jack Solomons took an alternative view. He announced that for his future promotions at Harringay he would invite leading American heavyweights over to the UK to face our rising stars in the hope that British victories would force America to accept them as legitimate challengers.

With Joe Erskine being the national champion, the British based Boxing News weekly trade paper had lifted him up to number nine in their world rankings, a fact that Nat Fleischer couldn't ignore given that he used roughly the same criteria when creating the ratings for the Ring. The American organisations had decided amongst themselves that the vacant title should be contested by light heavyweight champion, and Marciano's last victim, Archie Moore, against the much younger, Floyd Patterson. At that stage Levene, Solomons and the managers of Erskine and Cooper, not to mention Richardson and London, were beginning to visualise the potential opportunities.

Considering his recent performances, and the left hook emerging as a potent weapon, Wicks and Cooper must have been extremely confident of taming Bates, and this was reinforced in the very first round. A left hook flattened an overweight Bates, but he beat the count, staggering to his feet at nine. Henry backed off but gave the Derbyshire man a boxing lesson over the next three rounds. Disastrously for Cooper, during a couple of close exchanges he emerged with horrific cuts around both eyes. The Cooper team would later claim they were caused by Bates's elbow, but regardless, Henry was pulled out in the fifth round, and given the heavyweight picture being painted before the fight, this proved to be a major setback.

Cooper was on the sidelines for five months to allow his cuts to heal and while the time was passing the heavyweight picture moved on without him. In October Solomons kept to his plan and matched Richardson with the former top ten light heavyweight and heavyweight world champion, Ezzard Charles, at Harringay. The fight was an absolute stinker with Charles being disqualified in the second round for persistent holding.

The following month Patterson knocked out the veteran Moore to annex the title. Patterson's manager, Cus D'Amato was fiercely independent from the boxing organisations, the top promoters, and their Mafia backers. How this was ever allowed to happen remains a mystery, but he stood firm, and refused to allow Patterson to fight anyone he perceived to be connected with the mob. It also meant that Patterson's defences were not only few and far between, but not always against the top opponents.

Solomons maintained his ambitious programme, putting Richardson in with top ranked Cuban Nino Valdes in December. Valdes was a world class puncher and there were those who felt he'd been avoided by Marciano. He did have difficulty with quality boxers who weren't prepared to take chances against him, but that didn't apply to Richardson. The Welshman was given a going over and eventually stopped in the eighth round.

With Cooper and Erskine unable to fight for the British title due to injuries, Richardson being demolished, and London's manager declaring he was still not ready to challenge for titles, the year ended bleakly for what had been anticipated as an exciting period for British heavyweight boxing.

Even after the cut eye defeat by Bates, and the lengthy recovery period, Jim Wicks managed to secure not one, but two, titles fights within a short period of time for Cooper. The first of these would be an Empire title challenge to previous victim, Joe Bygraves, on another Solomons promotion at Earls Court in February, followed three months later with a European title attempt in Sweden against Ingemar Johansson.

On the same Earls Court bill, Erskine would face the devastating Valdes, and Solomons was keeping the press interested by talking up an open air fight in the summer between him and Henry, with both British and Empire, and possibly the European, titles on the line. It's easy to understand where the wily old promoter was going with all this. How could Patterson refuse to fight the holder of three titles?

The 19 February promotion turned into a disaster for all concerned. Henry plodded through his bout with Bygraves failing to stamp his superiority on the strong but limited Empire champion. As the fight progressed Cooper was cut over the left eye and under the right, while the crowd occasionally broke into slow handclaps. In the ninth round Bygraves floored Cooper with a body shot. Henry stumbled to his feet to beat the count, and was promptly dispatched to the canvas with an identical shot, and this time he couldn't recover.

Solomons must have been in despair with this outcome, because an hour earlier Erskine had been knocked out in under three minutes by Valdes. Six months previously, British boxing, and in particular leading promoters Jack Solomons and Harry Levene, believed that Erskine, Cooper or Richardson were capable of ending the search to find a heavyweight world champion from Britain to follow on from Bob Fitzsimmons whose reign ended some fifty eight years earlier. These hopes were now in tatters with Valdes destroying both Richardson and Erskine, and Cooper being stopped by a man who'd regularly been beaten whenever he stepped up a level.

In the dressing room after the Bygraves defeat the Cooper camp were in a very subdued mood. Henry could never explain why he'd performed so poorly. Many years later he'd suggest that whenever he went above 13st 7lb or thereabouts he felt sluggish and couldn't get his punches off. For the Bygraves fight he was half a pound under 14st, but he'd been slightly heavier before in his bout with Maurice Mols. It was also a common theme throughout his career that he certainly did not like to take shots to the midriff. In later fights he could be seen literally jack knifing backwards to avoid such punches. There can be no doubt this was a crushing blow to Henry's boxing aspirations. While he'd lost previously to Bacilieri and Bates, both defeats had resulted from cut eye retirements when he'd clearly been winning the fights, but this was a 'knockout' defeat in a bout he was probably losing. There has never been a clear explanation for this defeat but there was likely a combination of factors. While recovering from his injury he had to go back to his trade of plastering to ensure a steady income and when the Bygraves fight was arranged it is believed his training schedule had to start from 'scratch'. His principal sparring partner was his brother George, and although the brothers would regularly engage in 'wars', the variety was certainly missing. The extra half stone tends to suggest it was an abbreviated training regime.

Ingemar Johansson was a boxing enigma. He was disqualified for 'not trying' in the final of the 1952 Olympic Games and to watch him boxing thereafter enticed the onlooker to consider they were witnessing a novice fighter, or even an actor pretending to box on a film set. The reason for the extraordinary outcome at the Olympics and his 'visually' poor performances since was that he was basically a counter-puncher. Johansson either did not know how to attack effectively, or he was extremely patient and prepared to wait, as long as it took, for an 'opening' to appear. The problem for his opponents was that his right hand counter-punch, which came to be christened 'the Hammer of Thor', could poleaxe the most experienced and toughest opposition.

Since the Olympics four years previously Johansson had only engaged in sixteen contests, an unusually low number for fighters of that era. He'd won nine by knockout, one by disqualification and the rest on points. Joe Bygraves had managed to last the distance with him but Peter Bates had been stopped within two rounds. He'd won the European title from Franco Cavicchi by thirteenth round knockout in Rome.

Recordings of fights were extremely rare in those far off days, so managers and trainers had to rely on personal opinions of others. There can be little doubt that Jim Wicks consulted people who'd watched the Bygraves and Bates fights and they would have told him of the power in Johansson's right hand.

Henry's principal sparring partner, as usual, was brother George, while British middleweight Albert Finch assisted Johansson. With Cooper being surprisingly sluggish in his last outing against Bygraves, and coming off a cut eye defeat to Bates, there has to be some doubt in how confident he was going into this championship contest, in a foreign country, and with an assumption that his team had emphasized Johansson's punching power.

Perhaps all this pre-fight baggage contributed to what turned out to be a rather tentative performance form Cooper. For four rounds, in the evening sun of Stockholm, both men tiptoed around the ring throwing the occasional lacklustre jab. It seems obvious now that Cooper was wary of committing himself to attack knowing that this was part of Johansson's plan. With the Swede making no effort to step up the pace the referee stepped in and called for more action. Rather foolishly Cooper took the instruction to heart and walked straight into 'Ingo's bingo' which exploded onto Henry's exposed chin and he was down and out – gone!

Cooper said in the immediate aftermath he never saw the punch hitting him and didn't feel a thing. He believed he'd been knocked completely unconscious, although film of the fight showed him sitting near the ropes and trying to rise. Soon after, presumably after Jim Wicks had a word in his ear, Cooper suggested the setting sun blinded him, explaining why he didn't see the knockout punch approaching!

At the time, people didn't fully realise just how far Johansson's vaunted punch could take him. In fact he went on to win the world title smashing Floyd Patterson to the canvas seven times. Prior to that he'd knock out Joe Erskine and stunned world class Eddie Machen by knocking him out in under three minutes. There's always a great debate on whether knockout punchers are born or made. No one could have taught Johansson to punch like this. His right hand punch didn't even look particularly devastating, but it just seemed to be timed to perfection, and was extremely accurate. It's possible that his opponents, having got into the ring with him, were so surprised at how awkward he moved, that the 'fatal' punch just seemed to come out of nowhere, catching them unawares. Cooper's knock out defeat by Johansson, viewed from the present day, was not such a disaster as it appeared at the time.

Just over a week later, Erskine got back to winning ways with a points victory over Bates, which, strangely enough, was NOT for the Welshman's British title. We have to assume that either the Board didn't feel Bates was a worthwhile challenger, or they were holding to their original decision that the next defence must be against Cooper. The night before, Richardson failed to win the Empire crown from Bygraves, when their fight was adjudged a draw.

Although the heavyweight scene was looking a bit depressed, Brian London was storming up the ratings. Since his first round knockout defeat by Cooper, he'd fought six times, winning five by knockout and his solitary defeat was on points in Germany. This loss can be largely ignored given that a visitor struggled to win there, in fact the old adage that you had to knock your opponent out to get a draw just about sums things up!

Much against the views of the boxing press, Henry's next outing was in September, as the challenger for Erskine's Lonsdale belt. It was widely felt that either Richardson or London deserved the opportunity more, given that Cooper had now lost his last three fights.

The press were also critical of the preparations of both camps, in particular their choice of sparring partners. Erskine was using Alan Hand, Redvers Sangoe and Fred Powell. Hand and the light heavyweight Sangoe were light punchers with losing records while Powell was a veteran of some forty seven fights and had seen better days.

Henry's sparring partners were brother George, Terence Murphy and Dave Sammons. Murphy was a middleweight and Sammons was just starting out on a professional career, which ultimately did not last long. The press were probably correct in their beliefs in that none of the sparring partners mentioned could be relied on to take either boxer out of their comfort zone. Maybe both camps felt that as the opposition was so well known to each other, all that was needed was fine tuning!

There were big problems outside the ring for Erskine before the fight began. The

Welshman discovered his manager had been 'fiddling' his purse money and sacked him the night before the contest. Not the ideal preparation. He must have had a brass neck however, as he sat at ringside with the Boxing News reporter shouting instructions to his former protégé.

The fight was not a thriller in fact many at ringside felt it was nothing more than a glorified sparring session. Henry landed two left hooks in the first half of the fight which momentarily staggered the champion and he might well have been fractionally ahead at that stage. From then on until the end Erskine moved and parried, landing nice counters with very little power but point scoring nevertheless. At the final bell the referee awarded the contest to Erskine, but it'd been very close. Cooper himself reckoned that if he'd indeed lost it, there could only have been a round in it. The Boxing News gave it to the champion by a couple of rounds. Erskine now had two notches on the Lonsdale belt, and Henry was looking over a precipice.

Cooper's mentor and manager, Jim Wicks, was having a terrible time. For almost a year his stable of fighters didn't seem able to manage a worthwhile victory amongst them. Jake Tuli, his Empire bantamweight champion had lost that title, and the next four fights in a row; light heavyweight Alex Buxton lost a vacant British title challenge to Randolph Turpin and won only a single fight out of his next four; his British lightweight champion Joe Lucy lost the title to Dave Charnley and subsequently retired; Henry's middleweight sparring partner Terence Murphy lost a close fight for the Southern Area title and two fights later he retired; Percy Lewis lost to Hogan Kid Bassey in yet another Empire title challenge and further down the scale Wicks's remaining two fighters, Paddy Delargy and Eddie Wright, were also on losing runs. An incredible sequence of bad luck for the experienced manager.

Following the Erskine defeat, Henry had reached rock bottom. Only three years into what looked like a promising career he now had to seriously consider whether to continue or to go back to his trade as a plasterer. Cooper had been living the life. Training full time, watching what he was eating, not socialising like other young men and still living at home with his parents. While success in the ring and financial stability were motivating factors, four defeats in a row and three title challenges repelled must have caused the twenty three year old to ask himself if it was all worthwhile. Jim Wicks knew this and advised Cooper to take a month off to think things over.

Henry Cooper: Cut Eyes and Left Hooks

It was decision time for Wicks also, as far as Henry's career was concerned. He'd three options. He could advise Henry to retire, or he could take him down a route whereby he'd become an opponent for other aspiring heavyweights. There's no doubt Cooper could have been invited to America and all over Europe as well as back home in Britain, where he'd fight regularly for good money and provide a decent measuring gauge for anyone. Or he could rebuilt Henry's confidence and start again.

CHAPTER 3

Cooper Crashes the World's Top Ten

IN THE THIRD QUARTER OF 1957 THE BRITISH BOXING PRESS HAD WRITTEN OFF Cooper as a serious challenger for any of the major titles available. Joe Erskine was British champion and had defeated Cooper twice. Joe Bygraves was Empire champion and stopped Cooper in a defence earlier in the year. European champion Ingemar Johansson was scheduled to defend against Erskine, and he'd already destroyed Henry with one punch. In twelve months he'd become just 'another' heavyweight.

During October Cooper rested and thought hard about what he wanted out of boxing. Manager Wicks gave him breathing space and left the final decision down to him alone. Henry totally trusted Wicks, and as the future would show, his faith was well founded. Wicks never lost his confidence in Henry's ability, and the wily old manager understood the boxing game well. He knew talent when he saw it, but Henry needed to convince himself.

Wicks must have been a happy man when Henry let him know he was ready to get back into training, and lost no time in getting the train back on the rails. In recent years Wicks had become accustomed to taking his boxers over to the continent, particularly Italy and Germany, building up contacts as he went along. Wicks arranged a fight for Cooper in Dortmund against the German champion, Hans Kalbfell, and while they were preparing to leave Britain for the fight it was announced that Henry would be fighting Brian London the following month.

On 16 November in front of 8,000 German fans, Cooper was reborn. He totally dominated Kalbfell for the entire ten rounds landing incessantly with the left hand and drawing cheers of appreciation from the crowd. Between rounds six and nine the Boxing News correspondent at ringside counted thirty two solid left jabs and hooks landing flush making Kalbfell's face look a mess. There was no doubting the result, even in Germany, and at the end the German promoter was so impressed he

Henry Cooper: Cut Eyes and Left Hooks

offered Wicks a minimum purse of £2,000 to bring Cooper back in January. However, typically for Cooper in those days, every 'silver lining had a cloud'! He'd been cut again over the left eye, an injury which prevented the fight with London.

Determined to keep Cooper's name in the limelight, Wicks produced two gems for the journalists to eat up. He first of all claimed that a syndicate led by the then famous actor, Stanley Baker (of 'ZULU' fame) had offered Wicks £50,000 (£1.1 million today!!) to buy out his contract. Then he suggested that Henry was being treated by a psychologist in Germany who was teaching him how to relax. Cooper would later deny the syndicate story, but Wicks did have an outstanding gambling debt, and the person he owned the money to, wanted to write off the amount in exchange for Henry's contract. The second story was complete nonsense. Before the Kalbfell fight Cooper had met a local girl and struck up a relationship which necessitated the occasional trip to Germany. Both 'fibs' generated the required amount of free publicity and went some way to repair the damaged reputation.

The year came to a close with Erskine now holding both the British and Empire titles having recently beaten Bygraves. Brian London was exciting the fans imagination with his fearless attacking style and although Richardson was still ranked above Cooper, a series of defeats to decent American opposition was counting against him. Wicks, needing to keep Cooper's name in the frame, stuck to his continental plan by matching Henry in Germany on 11 January with Heinz Neuhaus.

Neuhaus was a former European and German champion, and in truth wasn't a bad fighter. Nevertheless there were clear patterns observable in his boxing record, if anyone cared to examine it closely. In fifty four fights he'd only ventured outside Germany on three occasions – all defeats! When foreign boxers with any sort of 'name' travelled into Germany they seemed to have great difficulty securing a win, all except the hard punching Cuban, Valdes, who couldn't have read the script. He knocked out Neuhaus in four rounds. Former British champion Johnny Williams was held to a draw then stopped a couple of years later. Joe Bygraves lost on a disqualification, the world ranked American Rex Layne was held to a draw, then defeated, and more recently both Peter Bates and Brian London had lost on points. These should all have been indications to the Cooper team as to what to expect if Henry's left hook failed to bring an early finish.

To be fair to Neuhaus, he put up a spirited performance, probably the last big effort of his long career, and he actually had Cooper down in the fourth round. Apart from the tenth and last round, when he made a great effort to try to swing the fight in his favour, all other rounds appeared to have been won convincingly by Cooper. However, the German judges unanimously declared the fight to have been a draw. The Boxing News reporter gave the fight to Cooper by a couple of rounds, and didn't seem too upset with the official result. Henry saw things differently, and couldn't believe he hadn't come away with a win.

Cooper learned later that the German commission employed a rather unusual method to score a fight. Each round had five points up for grabs, but if a fighter didn't win all the points in a round it was declared a draw. That explained a lot!

In February, Wicks and Cooper came to realise just how far off the pace he was with Britain's two foremost promoters, Solomons and Levene. 'Jolly Jack' matched Brian London with the world's number four ranked heavyweight, Willie Pastrano, in the hope that a victory for the Blackpool man would result in an elimination contest against either Eddie Machen or Zora Folley for the right to challenge the world champion, Floyd Patterson. Meanwhile Levene arranged for Patterson to come to London to appear in an exhibition bout on one of his future promotions. Joe Erskine travelled out to Sweden, in what turned out to be a forlorn attempt to wrest the European title from Johansson, while the British public anticipated a triple title fight between him and London over the summer should he manage to be successful.

Once again Britain's new heavyweight hopes were shot down in flames. London was outpointed by Pastrano although the decision was hotly disputed, and the light punching Erskine proved no threat to Johansson who steadily and systematically punched him to a standstill. Wicks must have had a wry smile with these results knowing that they would have done Cooper's status no harm whatsoever.

Even two good performances in Germany were not enough for Henry to retain his position as number one contender for Erskine's titles. The Board decided in early March that Brian London would face the champion in June, while Cooper was required to meet Dick Richardson in an eliminator. To keep their title moving the Board also decreed that whoever emerged victorious between Erskine and London would not get the usual six months grace before making a defence. They would need to meet the Cooper/Richardson winner in a much shorter period.

Levene and Solomons were now in open opposition to each other. The latter had

Henry Cooper: Cut Eyes and Left Hooks

ruled the roost for many years but Levene was determined to outflank him. He kept publicising his relationship with those managing Patterson's career, provoking Solomons to continue bringing over strong American opposition in response. Richardson was the man being put forward by Solomons, without much success, in the hope that the huge and aggressive Welshman would eventually come good. Since being knocked out by Valdes he'd been outpointed by both Pastrano and Bob Baker and was now matched with Cleveland Williams. Williams had already amassed forty one fights, losing only two, and thirty four of his victories coming by knockout. At that moment there was a strong argument to suggest that he, and not Patterson, was the best heavyweight in the world. Richardson, knocked down in the first, was disqualified in the fourth round after repeated warnings to keep his head up. Solomons plans had fallen apart once again.

Wicks was determined to keep Henry's career ticking over and he did this by taking him back over to Germany in April. In the opposite corner this time would be the German light heavyweight champion, Erich Shoeppner. He'd won twenty one fights on the spin and was being lined up by the Germans for a world title challenge to Archie Moore. To help appreciate again how difficult it was to get a verdict in Germany it's worthy of note that after this fight with Cooper, he would fight another seventeen times over the next five years in his homeland and remained undefeated throughout. On the first occasion he fought outside Germany, in his thirty ninth contest, he lost. Four months prior to that defeat, Schoeppner fought a draw with an American, Von Clay, after being knocked down three times!

The record books show that Cooper lost his fight with Schoeppner, having been disqualified in the sixth round. It's difficult to report accurately now on what actually transpired without the benefit of film footage. The Boxing News correspondent at ringside reported that Cooper was being outboxed over the first three rounds, and indeed the German floored Henry during this period. It appeared thereafter that Cooper picked up the pace after this setback and began dominating the home fighter. In the fateful sixth round Schoeppner bounced off the ropes towards Cooper and turned away. As he did so, Henry blasted him with a left hook behind the ear and he dropped like a stone. It transpired that Schoeppner was hospitalised for five weeks as a result of the blow. The referee turned to Cooper and raised his arm to signify he'd won the fight. It was only after much confusion and discussion between officials at ringside that the decision was reversed, and Cooper was disqualified. The Boxing News journalist claimed the decision to disqualify Cooper was entirely justified believing that Henry had become anxious due to being behind at the time of the stoppage.

A different story emerged from the Cooper team. Henry later said that Schoeppner was tiring and beginning to take a bit of a beating. When the fight ended Henry admits his opponent was turning away, but the left hook had already been on its way. To add insult to injury the German Boxing Board withheld half of Cooper's purse. Wicks would later claim that the German Board was virtually bankrupt and they needed to retain the money to remain solvent! Jim Wicks never forgave the German authorities for what transpired, an issue which may well have cost Cooper the European title in years to come.

On 3 June Henry learned who he'd have to meet for the British and Empire titles if he overcame Richardson, and surprisingly it wasn't his old foe Joe Erskine. The champion had been coping admirably well with the crude swings thrown by London until he suffered a cut left eyebrow in the seventh round. During the next round Erskine seemed to lose all concentration and allowed the Blackpool bruiser to launch attack after attack until the referee called a halt with Erskine failing to beat the count after being knocked down.

Many boxing historians have considered Cooper's three fights in Germany as the turning point in his career, and this is a valid argument, but Wicks and Cooper may not have appreciated this at the time believing, that as the Richardson fight approached, a defeat would certainly confine Henry to the status as an 'opponent' for the immediate future, if not indefinitely. He'd already lost three title challenges, twice by stoppage, and Levene and Solomons were not knocking doors down to have him on their promotions. Both promoters, and the boxing press, knew that Dick Richardson was limited, and if Cooper could not handle him then there could be no future for him at the top level. Although there is a debate about how exactly Cooper's last two fights in Germany should have been scored, the reality is that his official record demonstrated that he'd only one victory in his last seven contests.

Richardson was a giant of man in the heavyweight division for that era. At 6' 4" he was taller than every world heavyweight champion there had ever been, with the exception of both Jess Willard and Primo Carnera. He consistently weighed just under 15 stones, rarely carrying any excess fat. He could box and punch, but his downfall was that he didn't have a boxer's mentality. When he got caught he lost his temper and entered into 'street fight' mode. Every time he stepped up a level, he lost, often by way of disqualification due to some infringement of the rules when he lost his temper. Ten months before he fought Cooper for example, he'd taken on the top level American, Bob Baker. The fight had been slow and boring for five rounds as Richardson stuck to his game plan, throwing cautious jabs and little else – but he was winning the fight. In the next round, following slow handclaps from the crowd, the referee intervened and ordered more action. Baker opened up and Richardson went to pieces, losing the remaining rounds and the contest. Ominously for Henry however, Richardson had avenged that loss two months before their fight, and at the same venue as their forthcoming contest, on home turf for Richardson, at Porthcawl in Wales.

Cooper's preparations for the fight did not go all that smoothly. Wicks brought in a foreign sparring partner, an allegedly strong puncher who was expected to bring out the best in Henry. It wasn't often that Wicks's judgment was wrong. Cooper knocked the import out with two punches, and his brother George had to take over. During one typically vigorous sparring session George cut Henry over the eyebrow and the fight was postponed for a week.

As the publicity build up began, most of the specialist boxing press favoured Richardson. They cited the Welshman's extra height, the fact he was fighting on Welsh soil, and the higher level of opposition he'd faced during Cooper's sojourn in Germany. Most also felt however that if the fight went the ten rounds distance Cooper's boxing skills would most likely see him prevail. There's little doubt this was an intriguing match-up attracting huge interest given that boxing was the second most popular sport in the country, just behind football.

Henry knew Richardson well from their army days and knew what to expect. Then the Welshman was known as a bit of a bully who would often engage in street fights. The Cooper camp were also aware that he had a tendency to deliberately butt his opponents, and they felt this might be a tactic he'd use in the very first round in the expectation that a referee wouldn't disqualify him so early in a fight of this importance. They'd obviously done their homework well because this is exactly what happened. Richardson did indeed butt Henry, causing a vertical cut to appear, moving upwards from the eyebrow to the hairline. As soon as the home fighter saw the damage he went for broke throwing everything into an early victory. Cooper covered up well and weathered the storm allowing cutman, Danny Holland, to do his job in the corner.

The next three rounds were calmer affairs, with neither man taking control. In a dramatic fifth round Richardson landed a roundhouse right to the susceptible Cooper mid rift and the Londoner sank to the canvas. Henry looked to his corner and signalled he was unhurt. There was a belief among those at ringside, that Richardson, seeing the eye contact with his corner, misinterpreted the situation, and believing Cooper was seriously hurt, stormed towards his opponent intent on finishing the 'weakened' man. This turned out to be a massive misjudgement by Richardson if that was the case, because he walked onto a vicious left hook, one that Cooper always thought was his best ever punch. All those present in the press rows maintained the punch lifted the Welshman clean off his feet onto his back, and totally out cold. The fight was seen by thousands later on TV and gave birth to the almost legendary status of the Cooper left hook (later to be known as Henry's Hammer).

Although critical of Richardson's boxing ability and his losses to top level Americans, Cooper's stunning win can be put into some perspective when it's realised that eighteen months later the big Welshman annexed the European title in Germany, and successfully defended it three times, twice more on foreign soil.

With this result Cooper had recovered his early promise and needed only one more success, against Brian London, to establish himself as Britain's leading heavyweight out of the original quartet who set out in 1954.

CHAPTER 4

British and Empire Champion

FOLLOWING COOPER'S DEMOLITION OF DICK RICHARDSON IN A FINAL eliminator for Brian London's British and Empire heavyweight titles he was aware from the Board of Control's instructions that the fight had to take place within six months. Although winning the titles was important, a regular source of income also exercised his mind. Henry had become a full time boxer, and purses from his fights were now his only method of earning money. From manager Wicks's perspective there were ongoing expenses to meet, including rent for using the space he had for an office and gym at the Thomas a' Becket pub, as well as paying sparring partners. The last purse of £6,000 for the Richardson fight had been almost completely subsumed by these costs. So, a money earning fight prior to the London contest had become almost a necessity.

With Cooper's name now back in prominence, promoters Levene and Solomons were keen to engage his services. Over the previous three years they both had promoted ten fights between Britain's top heavyweights and leading American contenders for the world title now held by Floyd Patterson. Henry hadn't been included in any of them. Erskine, Richardson, Bygraves and London only managed three wins between them, and this included a cut eye victory for London over Willie Pastrano, and a disqualification success for Richardson against Ezzard Charles, who was basically a 'shot' fighter. Whatever the rival promoters were trying to achieve it certainly hadn't been successful up until then.

Towards the end of September 1958 it was reckoned the top three contenders for Patterson's crown were Archie Moore, Eddie Machen, and Zora Folley. These rankings had suddenly been altered by events in Stockholm, when much to the surprise of American experts, Ingemar Johansson once again swung the 'Hammer of Thor' this time on Machen's chin, within the first three minutes of their contest, leaving the perceived number two contender out cold.

Almost at the same time as news of that shock was reaching our shores, Harry Levene announced that he'd enticed Folley to Europe for the first time, to fight Cooper. The American was a real top level performer of that there can be no doubt. Standing around an inch shorter than Cooper but more heavily built, he'd fought forty five times in three years as a professional, winning an incredible forty one, with two draws and only two losses. His two losses came as retirements following a broken jaw and a broken rib. He could certainly punch, with twenty five wins coming inside the distance. As the fight with Henry approached the bookmakers had Folley as a two to one on favourite.

Years later Cooper would tell his biographer a very interesting story of how the fight came about. Henry was originally due to take on highly ranked Argentinian Alex Miteff, however he got injured during a previous fight and had to call off. Levene then called his American contacts seeking a top ten opponent. They offered Valdes and a 'new' name, Sonny Liston. While this was happening, and unknown to Levene, Wicks himself had contacted Folley's team and got an agreement with them. When Levene and Wicks sat down to discuss this, Levene put forward his two names. Wicks knew of Liston, and having seen Valdes in the flesh, wanted no part of either. The influential Ring Magazine now had Folley and Archie Moore locked as joint number one contenders, and Wicks insisted on meeting one or other knowing full well that Levene couldn't afford the purse Moore would demand. So the wily old manager got his way!

It's always been maintained that Wicks would never have agreed to a fight against Liston with the implication that he was too tough for Henry. On a previous visit to America Wicks had been warned, possibly by Chris Dundee, that if ever he was offered a fight against a 'guy' called Sonny Liston, he should avoid it at all costs. It's difficult to imagine that someone so astute as Wicks would suggest that a possible future opponent, perhaps even for the world title, was simply too good for his man. Perhaps Wicks's comments were a smokescreen for the real reason – the fact that Liston was heavily involved with the Mafia who controlled his career, and that no matter the circumstances Cooper would never get a fair deal.

The bout with Folley took place at the Empire Pool at Wembley in front of an estimated 9,000 fans. In the lead up to the fight Harry Levene was telling anyone who'd listen that if Cooper won he'd move heaven and earth to secure a world title fight with Patterson.

Henry Cooper: Cut Eyes and Left Hooks

During the opening exchanges of the first round Cooper looked supremely fit and was confidently coming forward throwing strong jabs, but Folley held his ground. It soon became obvious that Folley's team had done their homework on Cooper. On several occasions as Henry waded in, vicious right hand counters came flying over, not landing cleanly but with sufficient force for Henry to start backing off. The fight took a turn for the worse for Cooper in the third round. Those right hands began to land and the left eyebrow of Cooper burst open. This was all the incentive Folley needed and he began to move in. A solid right knocked Henry onto the ropes, and a flurry of lefts and rights ended with a 'cuff' across the back of the head putting Cooper down. He wasn't hurt, the knockdown was a mixture of a loss of balance and a need to escape the onslaught. Folley must have judged the situation perfectly because he failed to follow up his attack suspecting that Cooper had all his senses about him and might be waiting for a mistake on his part.

Once again Danny Holland worked his magic on the damaged eyebrow and Henry quickly got back to his usual routine, jabbing hard and repeatedly into the face of the visitor. As the fight progressed the huge crowd began to anticipate a famous British victory. When the bell sounded for the last round the crowd almost lifted the roof off as they cheered Cooper on. Folley made a last ditch attempt to land the right hand again but the forward momentum of Cooper ensured he couldn't set himself. At the final bell referee Little raised Cooper's hand, to signify his greatest win to date, and one that catapulted him into the world's top ten. The Cooper purse was £7,500 (around £160,000).

Three years later, Folley, who it has to be acknowledged seemed an honest enough person, would claim, when pressed, during an interview, that the time of this fight he was not in the best condition. He somewhat shyly said he took the fight at short notice and didn't have sufficient time to prepare, adding that his extra weight on the night supported his claim. There may be a bit of truth to his assertion. A month after the Cooper fight Folley was back in England to fight Joe Bygraves and weighed in half a stone lighter, a fight he won by ninth round knockout.

The world title scene had become a bit of a farce due to Cus D'Amato refusing to accept any challenger to Patterson who was perceived to have any connections with organised crime. As a consequence the champion had defended his title only three times in three years, and on one occasion against a man having only his first professional fight after winning the Olympic gold medal!

Shortly before Christmas, and being very much aware of these circumstances, Harry Levene and Johansson's manager travelled out to America to meet D'Amato in an effort to encourage him to allow a European challenger. Levene, one must assume, had either London or Cooper at the back of his mind.

While these negotiations were continuing in the background, the stage was now set for Cooper's fourth crack at a title in two years. Jack Solomons promoted the eagerly anticipated challenge for Brian London's British and Empire crowns at Earls Court on 12 January. In those far off days genuine animosity between boxers was a rarity, but this fight was an exception. In May 1956 Henry had knocked out London within a round, and it was well known that this had been his most enjoyable moment to date in a boxing ring due to London's previous thrashing of his twin brother.

London and his team were well aware of this background, but he was now the champion and had gained considerable experience since then. London had improved, and winning the titles had increased his confidence. In their last edition before the fight, the Boxing News made some interesting comments. They maintained their belief that given Cooper's previous losses in title bouts he was undeserving of yet another opportunity. Quite who was 'deserving', was a question they never approached. Secondly, they came out very emphatically in their pre-fight analysis and predicted that London would stop Cooper within six rounds. The headline above the article read, 'LONDON SHOULD WIN BEFORE THE HALF WAY MARK'. The correspondent felt Cooper would start off in the ascendency with his better boxing skills but London would soon press the action and overpower him. It was further suggested, possibly with some justification to be fair, that Folley might not have been at his best against Henry citing the American's improved performance against Bygraves. There was a quite obvious anti-Cooper sentiment in the article.

Author and writer Peter McInnes who'd been Cooper's boxing manager in the army knew him well and had followed his career closely in the professional ranks. He felt that Henry's tentative performances against Bygraves, Johansson and Erskine were due to a subconscious fear of the weak tissues around his eyes being cut when he was attacking. Wicks and Cooper were well aware of this concern, and McInnes's conclusion was probably not too far from the truth. Cooper's sense of honour and integrity wouldn't allow him to use that as an excuse – it simply wasn't in his nature. Henry would later suggest that in the year following the Erskine defeat, and the five subsequent contests, he'd managed to control his anxiety about the cut eye situation, being at long last able to trust Danny Holland's skills in the corner between rounds. The evidence to support this could clearly be seen in how he continued on the offensive in the fights with both Richardson and Folley following injuries to his eyebrows.

The fight with London turned out to be as good and thrilling as any boxing fan would ever wish to see. As Henry would admit many years later it was also the toughest in his entire fifty five fight career. Not only did he suffer from the bumps, bruises, cuts and muscle fatigue expected from a gruelling fifteen round heavyweight championship contest, but in the early hours of the following morning he had a sickening stomach pain associated with the effects of swallowing huge amounts of now congealing blood. He'd been swallowing the blood from a damaged nose since the second round.

Cooper boxed superbly from start to finish, throwing, and landing, hundreds of solid left jabs intermingled with punishing left hooks to the unprotected head and body of London. Occasionally they'd stop London in his tracks, but the brave Blackpool battler walked through them attempting to land his own strong left and right hooks. With the fight beginning to slip away from London he mounted a determined assault on Cooper in the middle rounds, temporarily stemming the tide and raising the hopes of his corner, who'd obviously told him he'd be unable to outbox Cooper.

The tenth round was crucial in that London, for the first time, was being forced repeatedly onto the back foot and becoming demoralised, even raising an unexpected smile on Cooper's face. At this point Henry's left eye was swollen, but surprisingly not cut. He was cut under the right eye however and London's face was battered and bruised.

As the fight entered its final stages Cooper seemed to have gathered a second wind and was up on his toes boxing to perfection. So confused and disorientated was the soon to be former champion, that at the end of the fourteenth round London walked over to Cooper and raised his arm in victory! Henry just glanced at London and walked back to his corner. The official verdict was only delayed another three minutes, that was when referee Ike Powell gave the decision to Cooper.

At long last Henry was the British champion, along with the lesser important Empire bauble. He'd retain both for ten years, making nine successful defences, before eventually voluntarily relinquishing them, while securing three Lonsdale belts in the process.

A film of the fight can easily be obtained, and a viewing of it supports the idea that Cooper, the genial gentleman outside the ring, could be vicious inside it, to the extent of perhaps being less than sporting. In the eighth round London's head came into contact with Cooper's face. The referee stopped the fight to warn London. As the bout resumed, London raised two gloved fists towards Cooper, an accepted method of indicating an apology. Henry briefly flicked out his left glove, touched London's, and simultaneously launched a determined left hook at the Blackpool boxer's exposed jaw. Fortunately London was able to block the punch. Technically this wasn't illegal at the time, it became so years later, but very few top level boxers resorted to that tactic. In interviews after his retirement Cooper would admit this had been a deliberate ploy on his behalf.

Immediately after the fight Wicks was interviewed for television and stated he'd already been offered £35,000 to challenge Floyd Patterson and after the performance against London he'd now be seeking £50,000. It did seem though that Wicks was being less than candid. By the end of January Patterson's manager had been summoned before the National Boxing Association in New York following concerns about his protege's recent defences, or lack of them! D'Amato told them his next defence would be in May or June and newspaper reports stated a contract had been signed for Patterson to defend against Johansson, who was to receive a £70,000 purse for the privilege. It would surely seem that if Wicks had indeed been offered a fight with Patterson his demand for a fee of £50,000 would have been acceptable to the promoters?

Cooper must have been wondering over the next few months where his career was heading. He quite rightly thought he might have been in line for a crack at Patterson himself but in February there was confirmation that contracts for a Patterson v Johansson fight had been completed. This announcement was a double blow to Cooper because, both a world, and now also a European title fight were out of the question.

Not long afterwards came the stunning revelation that Brian London would challenge Patterson BEFORE the Johansson fight. This bout was scheduled for Las Vegas, with the Blackpool man being refused permission to take part in the contest by the British Boxing Board presumably because they felt he was not a worthy challenger.

It seems fairly clear that Wicks had either demanded too much money for the bout with Patterson or had simply refused to accept the fight if it was to take place in America. Cooper never fought in America throughout his whole career and Wicks must have had some reluctance to take him there. There can be no doubt that for Wicks to have agreed to go to the States he would have demanded a huge payday. D'Amato, and potential promoters, must not have been willing to reach an agreement. The alternative was for Levene or Solomons to promote the contest in Britain, but with such short notice, this probably wasn't feasible. D'Amato in the end found a cheaper British replacement in the shape of Brian London, who was subsequently banned, as forewarned, by the British Boxing Board for accepting the fight against their will.

The ongoing negotiations, and the need to recover after a particularly tough fight, were undoubtedly the principal reasons why Henry had his longest period out of the ring since turning professional. There was possibly another reason – tax. Jim Wicks would later go into battle with the Inland Revenue over the method by which boxers had to pay their taxes. He argued that entertainers could submit their earnings on a yearly basis, but boxers had to pay their income tax after each fight. This later became an issue in relation to how many fights Cooper would have each year.

In May, a brave, but outclassed, London took Patterson to the eleventh round before being flattened by a straight right hand punch which left him lying on his back, as he was counted out. Patterson has not been treated too kindly by history, primarily due to his humiliating defeats at the hands of Sonny Liston, but he was an outstanding combination puncher, with a terrific 'dig' in each hand for someone his size, and it was no embarrassment for London to survive as long as he did.

Towards the end of that month Wicks was working hard to secure Henry's next contest. It was first mooted that he'd be fighting Canadian Yvon Durelle who'd recently lost a world light heavyweight challenge to Archie Moore. Durelle was known to put on weight between fights and it was initially thought he'd challenge Henry for the Empire crown. When that fell through, an Empire fight was signed and sealed for Leicester against Australian heavyweight Allen Williams. Hours after the contract was signed between Cooper and Williams' agent in Britain, the Australian took part in a fight for his national title and ended up getting himself injured! The Leicester promoters, Jacobs and Griffiths, desperate to keep their July show on track, then plumped for South African, Gawie de Klerk.

There are many reasons why a fight could be postponed, but a print union strike is not usually one of them. J & G, as the joint promotional company came to be known, had to abandon the 14 July date because they couldn't get posters and tickets printed due to the dispute. Another issue with regard to setting a new date was an almost catastrophic event in world boxing history, when against all the odds, Patterson, and hence America, lost control of the heavyweight title. On 26 June Ingemar Johansson knocked the local hero down seven times in the third round to be the first non-American boxer to hold the richest prize in sport for twenty five years.

The Johansson victory caused confusion on a number of fronts. There was speculation that a 'return fight' contract was in place. The European Boxing Union got in on the act by insisting the Swede relinquish their championship, alerting Jim Wicks to the possibility of taking that particular route. Once J & G promotions in Leicester heard of this idea, they quickly stepped in and published the fact they had Cooper's name on a contract for an Empire title defence. Eventually they were forced to transfer their interests to Welsh counterpart, Sir Lesley Joseph, who eventually promoted the Empire title fight in Porthcawl on 26 August.

Henry was not impressed with the venue! It was situated in the middle of what could be described in modern parlance as a 'theme park', and Cooper would later say it was a 'dump'. The changing rooms were in a corrugated iron hut and with the weather being extremely warm it felt like an oven. The first few rounds of the fight reflected the fact that Henry hadn't fought for a while. He was slow and tentative allowing the South African policeman to swing huge overhand rights without fear of retaliation. One of these opened up yet another cut, this time under the left eye, but it didn't unduly concern the champion. The fifth round turned out to be the end for de Klerk. Referee Eugene Henderson broke the boxers from a clinch, and as was becoming a bit of a habit of Cooper, he immediately threw a vicious left hook catching the challenger by surprise and knocking him down. On arising he was met with two left hooks to the head and body and sank to the canvas again. The brave visitor rose for a second time to be met by a Cooper onslaught forcing the referee to intervene but not before the poor man's jaw was broken. Many at ringside felt the stoppage came far too late.

The stage was now set for Cooper's first defence of the British title against old foe, Joe Erskine.

Chapter 5

Erskine Defeated at Last

GIVEN WHAT WAS TO COME, IT'S DIFFICULT TO BELIEVE THAT TOWARDS THE end of 1959, even allowing for the fact that Cooper was British and Empire champion, he was probably not the most famous or popular boxer in this country. That's not to suggest he wasn't liked, of course he was, but a much smaller man, lightweight Dave Charnley held the boxing public's imagination at the time. The fans were attracted to an attacking fighter with a big punch, capable of knocking out the very best, and Charnley fitted the bill perfectly. The 'Dartford Destroyer' was approaching a world title challenge in Texas, attracting a great deal of attention.

Setting aside the upcoming Charnley fight, Henry's battle with Joe Erskine at Earls Court on 17 November was still anticipated with some relish, especially since the light punching Welshman had already beaten Cooper twice in the professional game.

Preparations began early, with Erskine moving his training camp from Cardiff to Leicester where he honed his skills at the Shaftesbury Boys Club gym. Cooper opted to change his routine. His team moved lock stock and barrel to the George Inn at Wraysbury, Buckinghamshire. All the pre fight speculation focussed on whether Erskine's boxing skills would once again be too much for the more powerful punches of Cooper.

Since they last met Erskine had beaten Bygraves, lost his titles to Brian London, been stopped by Johansson and had come back with four straight points wins, including one over Willie Pastrano. At the time of this fight the Boxing News had Cooper as the number two challenger to world champion Johansson, just behind Floyd Patterson, with Erskine at number six. In many people's eyes this was viewed as an eliminator for the world title.

Cooper, who knew Erskine well from their National Service days, always said the former champion was a shrewd operator. Even when Henry landed flush with his best punches both in amateur and professional contests, the Welshman's expression never altered. This caused Cooper to hesitate, not really knowing whether Erskine was 'drawing' him in to making a mistake, or if in fact he'd been hurt. It's puzzling trying to analyse Erskine's status as a top heavyweight from that era. There's no doubt he could read a fight well. His timing was good, he moved fluently around the ring and seldom seemed flustered. He knew when to attack and when to defend. He simply couldn't punch. The punches he threw looked good enough but they just seemed to have no effect on the opposition, and a heavyweight with a weak punch was never going to have a great deal of success.

In this fight the boxing purist could see why Cooper had so much difficulty with Erskine. Joe moved constantly around the ring to Cooper's right, always out of range of his left jab and vicious hooks. When the challenger stopped moving he attacked Cooper with left jabs and right crosses with his forward momentum carrying him into a clinch, tying up Cooper, and waiting for the referee, Eugene Henderson, to break them up. This was different to how Richardson and London approached their fights with Cooper. Both tended to stand in front of Henry trying to get their own punches off and invariably been too slow to avoid those coming back at them. Erskine was a much more thoughtful fighter.

Most people remember the fight due to the horrific ending in the twelfth round. From the tenth round there were signs that Henry was at last beginning to take control, and during the eleventh Cooper was loading up with his left hooks, some of which were landing solidly. This pattern continued into, what was to prove, the final round when Erskine finally succumbed, and dropped to the canvas. He seemed well aware of his surroundings and rose on steady legs. This time Cooper knew that he'd hurt Erskine and went after him with all guns blazing and it wasn't long before Joe was put down again – heavily.

Joe scrambled to his feet for the second time and Henry caught him with a left and right on the chin. It was obvious afterwards that at this point Erskine was semi-conscious and was just beginning to fall forward when Cooper, in full flow, landed a brutal left uppercut which lifted the stricken fighter off his feet. He flew backwards landing with the small of his back resting on the bottom rope and his head supported by the ring apron. It was an agonising scene. The referee seemed to move Cooper back to a neutral corner while everyone at ringside looked on in horror. There was an uncomfortable delay before an observer at ringside, followed closely by Erskine's corner men, rushed to his aid. They pulled him back through the ropes and he lay motionless for a few minutes before he thankfully recovered consciousness. Henry was blameless, he done his job, but in hindsight questions have to be asked of the referee's decision making.

There were two incidents during the fight, which tarnish Henry's public image. Midway through the first round Erskine bundled forward throwing a jab and right cross as he did so. Both missed the target but as he tried to grab hold of Cooper, he stumbled and fell down on one knee. The referee began to move in as Erskine was rising. When he got to his feet with his arms by his side, Henry threw a left hook at full power landing on the point of Erskine's totally exposed jaw, knocking him flat on his back. Henderson, for all his age and experience moved Cooper back to a neutral corner and began a count! Erskine meanwhile, showing his recuperative powers early in the fight, managed to struggle back to his feet. Boxers are told repeatedly to protect themselves at all times during a fight, but in this instance it's difficult to justify Henry hitting an opponent who at that precise moment was defenceless.

At the end of the fifth round a similar incident occurred. On this occasion the balance of doubt might well swing in Cooper's favour. Henry was on the attack and Erskine was backing into the ropes. The bell rang and Cooper landed another full blooded left hook on Erskine's chin as the Welshman's hands were coming down. The old film of the fight, with sound, seems to indicate the bell ringing at the exact time the punch was being thrown. What seems to challenge that scenario however is that Erskine appears to have begun to relax, suggesting he'd heard the bell before Cooper threw his punch. As the next round started the referee brought both boxers together and issued a warning.

As the 'swinging sixties' decade began, Cooper was in a very strong position to significantly advance his career. He'd successfully defended his British and Empire titles, and in the process had now convincingly beaten all reasonable challengers available. In February the influential Ring Magazine listed Henry as the number four contender for Johansson's crown, behind Folley, Patterson and Sonny Liston. Folley, having previously lost to Cooper, could only have been rated so highly due to a recent win over Eddie Machen. Of course, the 'real' nemesis for all contenders was the brooding figure of Liston, who was being systematically avoided by both Patterson, and then Johansson.

The European Boxing Union eventually stripped Johansson of their title and surprisingly it was Dick Richardson who got the nod to fight Hans Kalbfell, another Cooper victim, for the vacant championship. It can only be assumed that Jim Wicks had made it clear he wasn't interested in fighting for the continental bauble, and was pursuing a different route. To support this claim, there were reports that Johansson's team were becoming frustrated at the lack of progress in finding a promoter for the return bout with Patterson, and fighting Cooper was fast becoming an alternative option. This possibility would not have escaped Wicks's notice. However, when the Johansson and Patterson promotion issues were eventually resolved, with the fight scheduled for 20 June, Henry was now, once again, left high and dry.

As the year progressed the outlook for Cooper didn't improve. The dogged persistence of Dick Richardson paid off when he stopped Kalbfell to win the European title. It then seemed obvious that Richardson would fight Cooper with all three titles on the line, but Richardson was committed to fulfilling dates during the summer at Porthcawl. The one bright spot for Henry was his marriage to his new wife Albina in January and their delayed honeymoon might well have been timed for the summer in the mistaken belief that a world title opportunity might have been on the horizon. Then in June and July that avenue closed for the foreseeable future.

Patterson became the first heavyweight to regain his title when he wiped the floor with Johansson, and negotiations began as soon as the fight ended for a third meeting. Then a month later 'big, bad' Sonny Liston, the shadow hanging over world heavyweight boxing, came into the light, knocking out Zora Folley making it virtually impossible for either Patterson or Johansson to avoid him.

Meanwhile Richardson's management team secured a European title defence against Brian London, with the European Boxing Union ordering the winner to face Kalbfell. These arrangements forced Jim Wicks to take the 'American' route, a programme he'd avoided, with the exception of the Folley fight almost two years previously.

First up was a fairly safe bout on 13 September with Roy Harris. Harris came from the small town of Cut 'n' Shoot in Texas but the 'rough and tough' cowboy image which the name implies didn't describe Roy's fighting style. Harris had climbed the ladder with good solid wins over Bob Baker, Willie Pastrano, Willi Besmanoff and Joe Bygraves, resulting in a slightly undeserved opportunity to fight for Patterson's crown in August 1958. He retired in the twelfth round of that challenge and when the Cooper fight came around his world ranking had all but disappeared.

In April he'd been annihilated in the first round by Liston and two months later was knocked out in the fifth stanza by unheralded Canadian, Bob Cleroux. To be fair to Harris, when he came over to Britain for the Cooper fight, he hadn't quite accepted he was on the road out. When he weighed in, he was almost a stone lighter than when he fought both Liston and Cleroux, and was at his lightest weight for over three years. He was obviously fit.

At Wembley, Harris put up a brave show. He jabbed and grabbed until referee Jack Hart eventually had to warn him. Cooper boxed cleverly thumping in hooks when he could, but it was not until the eighth round that they paid off. Harris had been staggered on a couple of occasions beforehand but in that round he couldn't keep Henry off and was knocked to the floor. He rose at six and was hounded around the ring, just managing to survive the round. Harris lasted the full distance losing on points. All in all it was a good night's work for Cooper. He'd earned a good payday, got his name back in the public domain after ten months absence, beaten a 'recognised' opponent and but for a small cut on the vulnerable left eyebrow, emerged unscathed.

Richardson meanwhile successfully defended his European title against London but was now committed to the return fight with Kalbfell. Jack Solomons made a good offer to Wicks and Benny Jacobs (Erskine's manager) for another fight between the two in the springtime, but Cooper's manager was holding out to see what would become of the world title scene. Once again, the Johansson and Patterson re-match was initially postponed and this forced Wicks to accept the fight with Erskine. There seemed little point in delaying matters to the spring, so the contest was arranged for 6 December at Wembley.

The Cooper team took themselves back to Wraysbury in preparation, based in a nice bungalow backing onto the river. Accompanying Cooper again were Wicks, his brother George and Danny Holland, and along with them was another boxer in Wicks's stable, Percy Lewis, who'd an Empire title defence looming. Erskine had taken himself back to home turf in Wales, instead of Leicester, and it was there that disaster struck, when he injured a hand, and had to pull out. The promoter's nightmare had struck again!

Solomons set about finding a suitable replacement to keep his big show alive, and he didn't do Henry any favours when he came up with the American based Argentinian, Alex Miteff. Miteff had been scheduled to be Cooper's original opponent when he'd fought Folley in October 1958 and was undoubtedly a stiffer test than Erskine.

The New York resident was about the same height as Henry but much heavier. From twenty nine fights he'd won twenty three and drawn one. Miteff had been fighting regularly beating top level opponents including Besmanoff, Valdes, and Wayne Bethea. In recent times he'd drawn in Canada with rising prospect George Chuvalo and lost narrowly on points to both Eddie Machen and Zora Folley. For this fight Miteff came in half a stone heavier than normal suggesting he might not have been in full time training when he got the call. Having made that point it's worth remembering that Miteff was ranked as the world's number seven contender at the time.

Cooper carried on from the Harris fight with another dominant performance. He boxed superbly, firing out the left hand repeatedly, never giving Miteff a chance to get a foothold in the fight. With Henry running down the clock in the last round, knowing the fight was won, his lack of concentration allowed the Argentinian to land a big left hook, and Henry was knocked down and almost out. Fortunately for all concerned he had the sense to take his time on rising from the count, waiting until his head cleared a fraction, and got on his toes for the remainder of the round to secure another important victory.

The Cooper family could now enjoy a pleasant holiday over Christmas and New Year in the knowledge that his first outing in 1961 would be against Erskine in the postponed double title defence. In the February edition of the Ring Magazine they would annually produce their world rankings, which due to publication timings, were always two months behind, meaning that at the end of the previous year, Patterson was champion, followed by Liston, Johansson, Machen, Folley and Cooper.

CHAPTER 6

First Lonsdale Belt, but Disaster Follows

BRITISH BOXING WAS IN AN UNUSUALLY STRONG POSITION WHEN 1961 ARRIVED. For the first time in living memory Britain had a boxer listed in the world's top ten of all eight weight divisions. The 'big 'stars at the time were the 'crashing, bashing' middleweight, Terry Downes, and the man soon to challenge for a world crown a second time, lightweight Dave Charnley.

Even though Cooper's fight with Erskine had yet to take place, the boxing press were already predicting a 'triple crown' affair between Cooper and Richardson, should the latter be successful in his return bout with Kalbfell. In the background, Jim Wicks was still in discussions with both the Patterson and Johansson camps in the hope of securing a world title challenge. Henry was even hinting to some journalists that if he secured such a bout, the money he'd earn would probably be enough for him to retire.

Prematurely as it turned out, the Boxing News were encouraged to speculate who would be the new crop of heavyweights to replace Cooper, Erskine, London and Richardson and they were already predicting that one of this new breed would be the West Ham amateur, Billy Walker.

On 21 March Cooper and Erskine did eventually meet for the fourth time as professionals, and quite how Joe believed he could overcome Henry was anybody's guess. In the last fight it was clear to anybody watching that Erskine didn't have the power to cause Cooper problems. Being aware of this meant that Henry could simply attack at every opportunity without fear of reprisal, and the Welshman's camp would just have to pray for Cooper's vulnerable eyebrows to open up. Erskine had managed two wins since their last meeting, against fairly mediocre opposition, and there was nothing he had shown in them to suggest an upset.

Of the utmost importance for Henry in this fight was the chance to win a coveted Lonsdale belt outright, with a third British title fight victory. It was quite amazing to learn that the belt he could win had been made originally in the 1930s for another Welshman, Tommy Farr. Farr had gained a first notch on the belt in March 1937, but never defended it, and no one since had won the requisite three fights to claim it as their own. It was a unique item being made of pure gold.

The contest went the way of the informed predictions. Henry totally dominated proceedings landing left jab after left jab on the poor face of Erskine. The carnage lasted for five rounds and by the conclusion both Erskine's eyes were bleeding and shutting rapidly, adding to a suspected broken nose. The challenger's team pulled him out at the end of that round.

A week before the Erskine fight, Patterson had finally seen off Johansson with a conclusive sixth round knockout. By this time there was huge pressure building for Patterson to defend against Liston. The man whom Cassius Clay would later christen the 'big, ugly bear' had knocked out everyone except Eddie Machen. D'Amato, Patterson's manager, would delay this defence for an incredible eighteen months. The only top contender Liston hadn't beaten was Cooper, so it would be natural to believe that a 'final eliminator' was the obvious course, if D'Amato was so determined to avoid a clash with his fighter. Jim Wicks had made it abundantly clear this was never going to happen.

It's now been established that during this period Wicks was in direct discussions with D'Amato for a Patterson fight, but for some unknown reason this just didn't materialise. Like most similar situations in boxing, then and now, it's likely that money was the cause. Looking back now it's fairly obvious that D'Amato sensed Liston would prove too much for Patterson, and was trying everything within his power to prolong the inevitable, while still bringing in good money.

Wicks, and therefore, Cooper, were caught in the trap. Wicks wasn't prepared to give the go ahead for a triple championship fight with Richardson while there was still a chance of a scrap with Patterson, hence the reason the Welsh European champion didn't defend for almost a year.

Eventually Wicks was forced to accept he'd been out manoeuvred when he learned that Patterson was going to defend against Tom McNeeley in December. Not to be outdone Jack Solomons arranged another bout for Cooper on the very same night as Patterson's defence against his lightly rated challenger. There is no way of knowing now what Solomons and Wicks were planning when they sat down to discuss who would face Henry. They could have chosen a fairly safe opponent from America and achieved the aim of keeping Cooper in the limelight with the power brokers across the pond. Or they could've continued to enhance his standing as a leading contender by facing someone like Eddie Machen. Henry was still rated at number three behind Liston and Johansson, with Machen just behind him. With a Liston fight off the cards, and Johansson considering retirement, Machen appeared most suitable.

It was a shock therefore when Solomons announced that Cooper would go over old ground by facing Zora Folley. Journalists asked Wicks why he chose Folley over Machen, given that he'd already beaten the former, and he quite correctly pointed out that Folley had already beaten Machen. There was logic in the argument and Wicks must have been very confident that Henry would repeat his previous victory.

Hindsight has twenty-twenty vision and it's easy now to criticise Wicks, but it's difficult to understand why such a shrewd operator, as he was, should quite literally throw all his eggs in the one basket, when there was no necessity. A Cooper win would simply underline what he'd already established, that he could beat a leading contender. A loss however, would relegate Henry in all the world rankings, and knock him right out of the picture in terms of challenging Patterson.

There were three important factors also at play as the fight approached. In the three years since they last fought, Folley had 'went to the well' sixteen times to Henry's six. So would Henry be fresh and Folley stale?

Folley had won fourteen of these fights losing only by knockouts to Liston and the lightly regarded Alejandro Lavorante, but had beaten Miteff, Bygraves, Machen and Besmanoff, twice.

Another issue was Cooper's training regime. Up to this point, when Henry was preparing for a big fight, he left home for around five weeks with his team including Wicks, George and Danny Holland. He'd gotten into a routine where he was observed closely, without distractions, and it was fairly easy for him to continue here he'd left off. In these circumstances Henry simply buckled down to the task in hand knowing that the fight would arrive soon enough and he could then return home.

For the first, last and only time in his entire championship career Henry decided (or did Wicks allow him) to stay at home, travelling daily from Wembley into the Thomas a' Becket gym. Unknown to anyone but himself, Henry later revealed that he would occasionally take a look out his bedroom window when the alarm went off around 4am, turn over, and go back to sleep instead of going out on his morning runs.

It would also come to light, that a partial reason for the delay of nine months between the Erskine defence and the fight with Folley, was a problem Cooper had developed with his over worked left shoulder. Henry had been experiencing pain from shoulder to fist for some time but now it could no longer be ignored. He was sent to a sports injury specialist who recognised the extensive wear and tear damage and diagnosed it as a form of arthritis. The specialist went further and suggested that this would end his boxing career far quicker than his susceptible eyebrows.

Wicks didn't make many mistakes with Cooper's career but this was going to be one of them. Knowing that Folley had been fighting, and winning regularly, knowing Henry had problems with his shoulder, he agreed to a change in his training routine, even though he'd be fighting a man rated in the top five in the list of contenders for the world title. It was a risk too far, and it backfired spectacularly.

The fight didn't last long enough for anyone in the Cooper team to decide for certainty if the arthritic shoulder or the changed training routine were factors, but there was enough for them to realise that Folley was certainly at the top of his game. The American camp were well aware of how Cooper would fight. They knew he didn't particularly like body shots and struggled when pushed onto the back foot. The very first punch Folley threw was a long straight left to the mid section.

For the entire first round Folley came forward throwing big overhand rights causing Henry to be tentative with his own jabs and forcing him backwards. A small cut was even opened over the vulnerable Cooper left eye and the observant spectator could see Folley waiting to time a big right hand over the top of the Cooper jab. From the very first bell Henry had been taken out of his stride.

Cooper had an experienced corner team, and at the start of the second round it was clear what he'd been told to do. He began circling more, and tried to push forward with a double jab when he could. Midway through the round a jab fell short and Folley pounced. A huge overhand right landed flush on the side of the exposed Cooper chin, and he was gone. Bravely Henry managed to get onto one knee, through experience as opposed to any rational thought, and rose just as the referee counted him out. For a few moments Cooper staggered about the centre of the ring not realising what had actually happened. Even as Danny Holland took his gumshield out Henry was still totally bewildered.

The humble victor merely made his way back to the corner and was helped on with his dressing gown. Both boxers were interviewed in their respective dressing rooms after the fight. This was when Folley made the claims about his lack of preparation for their previous fight. He knew that Cooper had taken his number one ranking away then and that before this fight he'd been placed at number six. He hoped this win would lift him to a challenging position to fight Patterson.

The Cooper dressing room was packed with family, friends and journalists. Usually, Henry, in victory or defeat, was meek and mild when interviewed, but on this occasion there was an undercurrent of anger or resentment in Cooper, and Wicks, unusually for him, had little to say. It came out much later that Wicks had 'words' afterwards with Henry's wife, Albina, about the demands of the 'boxing business' and made it clear to both her and Henry that in future he would return to the former routine prior to major contests.

If a graph had been drawn reflecting Henry's career up to this point, the Folley loss created a very deep trough indeed. Not as deep perhaps as the one he was in after his consecutive losses to Bates, Bygraves, Johansson and Erskine but that was only because he now held the British and Empire titles.

When the Ring Magazine produced their new heavyweight placings it read as follows: Patterson, Liston, Machen, Folley, Lavorante, Cleroux, Johansson, Williams, Cooper, Clay and Logan.

It's worthwhile to consider Cooper's status following the crushing Folley loss. He was twenty seven years old. He'd earned a fair amount from boxing, enough to buy a nice house of his own for his wife and young family. He'd won a Lonsdale belt outright, and was reasonably well known and respected. On the other side of that coin he'd an injured left arm, he'd lost badly to a man he'd already overcome, and crashed down the world rankings, making the hope of a world title fight seem like a pipe dream. The only sensible fight on the horizon would have been a European challenge to Dick Richardson who was already committed to defending in Germany in a few months time. It wouldn't have been a huge shock if he'd retired there and then.

Nevertheless, the partially hidden anger in the dressing room following the Folley fight, only emphasized a clear determination within Cooper to get back up the ladder. Similar to the situation he was in when Wicks took him to Germany for his three 'make or break' fights, it was clear his manager would have to use all his skills if Henry was to quickly recover lost ground.

CHAPTER 7

Cooper Dominates British Heavyweight Scene

If 1961 ENDED IN DISASTER FOR COOPER LEAVING HIM PONDERING HIS FISTIC future, the following year would see him as a virtual spectator as the boxing world moved on without him. In September Sonny Liston did what everyone predicted and smashed Floyd Patterson to pieces in just over two minutes. Prior to that, following an excellent defence of his European title in Germany against Karl Mildenberger, Dick Richardson would succumb to the iron fist of Ingemar Johansson bringing a conclusive end to the possibility of a lucrative triple title fight with Henry.

The year began for Cooper with no plans in sight. Then, unexpectedly, he was presented with an opportunity to get back in the ring. Levene had a promotion arranged for 23 January at Olympia featuring world middleweight champion Terry Downes, in a 'warm up' fight for the world title. A week before the fight Downes called off, and Levene worked furiously to find a suitable replacement in an effort to keep his show alive. Astonishingly the promoter's matchmaker Mickey Duff found the current British and Empire heavyweight champion ready, willing and able to step into the breach against an as yet unknown American opponent. Henry was always in training, viewing it as a responsibility to ensure he never got too far out of condition, only stepping it up when a contest was arranged.

A few days before his fight, the excitement being generated focused more on the opponent's manager than the fighter himself. That was because the manager turned out to be none other than the former undefeated heavyweight champion Rocky Marciano. The boxer was Tony Hughes!

Hughes was based in Cleveland and had a deceptively impressive record of twenty four wins, but when he was eventually stepped up against a quality opponent in his last fight, he'd been outpointed.

On the night of the contest, after the fans had surrounded Marciano in search of autographs and photos, the living legend took his jacket off and went into the corner with his fighter. Hughes came storming out catching Cooper on the chin with a left hook and for the remainder of the round showed little respect for the British champion as he continued to throw wild hooks. Over the next few rounds Henry began to put some 'meat' into his punches and opened cuts around the eyes of his limited foe. Towards the end of the fourth round, as Hughes ducked low, a wicked left hook knocked him down for a count of seven but the bell rang before Cooper could finish him off. The end was in sight however, for in the next round Henry loaded up and slammed in left hooks and the occasional right cross causing most in the crowd to encourage the referee to bring a halt to proceedings. Between the fifth and sixth rounds Hughes's cornermen called the referee over and pulled their man out.

Cooper was back in action a month later this time in Manchester where he'd been beaten on cuts by Peter Bates almost six years previously. That fight had been the first in the disastrous four fight losing sequence, and all concerned were hoping that history wouldn't repeat itself. In the opposite corner was Wayne Bethea. The native New Yorker was in many ways the ideal opponent for Cooper at the time. He was a very experienced heavyweight who'd literally fought the best around for the last six years being stopped only by Sonny Liston. Zora Folley, Eddie Machen, Nino Valdes, Cleveland Williams, Alex Miteff, Ernie Terrell, Karl Mildenberger and Joe Bygraves were all on his record. He'd two split decision losses to Folley and one to Valdes. On the other hand he'd stopped Bygraves and outpointed Terrell. All the others were points defeats. Perhaps this should have been the type of opponent Cooper had fought instead of Folley in December.

The Bethea contest proceeded along a similar fashion to the Miteff bout fourteen months earlier, but without the shocking knockdown in the last round. Cooper jabbed and jabbed while Bethea throw overhand rights without ever landing cleanly. The sixth and ninth were convincing rounds for Henry when, unusually, his right crosses came into play causing the American serious problems. It was an emphatic, though uninspiring, points victory leaving the Mancunian fans disappointed.

Years later Henry would remember that by now, not only was his left shoulder giving him problems, but the elbow and fist were also damaged. Of course this was never mentioned to anyone outside the tight circle of confidants surrounding him. The injuries must however have affected his training regime considerably. If Cooper's major asset was his left jab and hooking with the same arm then it would be natural to work on these strengths during his training sessions. However, if continued use was exacerbating the problems it seems logical to assume that he'd spend less time using the injured arm. It really was a typical 'Catch 22' situation. The regular use of cortisone injections for ailments like arthritis began in the 1950s, and they would have provided temporary relief to Cooper if they had been used. It's not known if Cooper used this treatment but it had become reasonably common amongst footballers with troublesome knee problems.

The British and Empire heavyweight title had been lying dormant for over a year probably due to the only worthwhile challenger, Dick Richardson, being otherwise engaged defending his European crown. Since losing his world title challenge to Patterson, Brian London had been stopped by Richardson, Valdes and Machen. It seemed the only option was a Cooper defence against old foe, Joe Erskine, who since his last defeat from Henry had travelled to Canada where he'd secured a disqualification win over George Chuvalo. As the old guard from the mid fifties were beginning to fade the new breed were emerging in the shape of Billy Walker who was about to make his professional debut amid great publicity, and the Midlands hopeful, Johnny Prescott.

Soon after the Bethea fight, promoter Reg King announced that Cooper would indeed defend against Erskine at Nottingham Ice Rink on 2 April. The fact that neither of the big London promoters was involved perhaps demonstrated the comparative lack of interest in a fifth contest between the pair.

Despite the familiarity between them it turned out to be a decent battle, undoubtedly due to persistent attacks from Erskine. From the first bell he went on the offensive and stopped Cooper getting a foothold in the fight. Henry could be seen to be deploying his right hand much more and one of these opened a gash over Erskine's left eye. Joe had already been cut over his other eye from as early as the first round. Erskine kept up the pace and although Cooper might have been in front they're didn't seem to be much in it. By the ninth round however Erskine's left eyebrow was a jagged mess and without the punch power to halt Cooper, it had become a hopeless task. Between the ninth and tenth rounds Glasgow referee Frank Wilson inspected the damage and had no option but to end matters there and then.

After two years, in which Cooper had fought only four times, he'd now taken part in three fights in three months, a schedule he'd not undertaken since 1955. This was very much reminiscent of Wicks's plan to rebuild Henry with the trips to Germany after the infamous run of defeats. The three recent wins, however, hadn't improved his stock in world terms. The Boxing News had lowered him to the number eight contender position, a drop of two places, as had the Ring Magazine.

In June, Jim Wicks and Henry, travelled to Sweden, and saw Johansson knock out Richardson in the eighth round to regain the European title. Within days of that outcome the British Boxing Board wrote to the European Boxing Union insisting that Johansson should defend against Cooper. The Board certainly seemed determined to keep Henry active because a month later they instructed him to defend his British and Empire crowns against Richardson before the end of October.

There's no doubt the British fight scene had began to take a downward turn. Jack Solomons' influence was on the wane. Terry Downes lost his world middleweight crown and Charnley was slipping down the world rankings. At heavyweight, Joe Erskine seemed to be heading towards the exit door, Richardson, too, looked to be nearing the end, as did Brian London, although the latter would surprise everyone, and was still competing eight years later. Walker, Prescott and newcomer, Jack Bodell, were receiving a lot of publicity, but any thoughts of a British heavyweight challenging for the world title anytime soon, had long gone.

Sonny Liston was now the world champion and there were many who firmly believed he was unbeatable. In the meantime Cooper's inactivity since April, saw him drop further down the world rankings, as a new young star was making plenty of waves – Cassius Clay.

Finally, Harry Levene announced that Henry would defend both his titles against Richardson on 13 November, and the champion promptly set up camp once again at the George Inn in Wraysbury. Perversely perhaps, Richardson based himself at the Thomas a' Becket, Cooper's backyard!

When the date of the fight arrived Cooper had dropped out the world's top ten listings completely, and there was further bad news just around the corner. For the first time, Wicks was forced to tell a promoter his charge had to pull out, citing the reason as a damaged elbow.

The previous year ended in disaster, and 1962 had proved only slightly better given he'd achieved three wins and gained a notch on a new Lonsdale belt. Tarnishing this success was the fact that Cooper had now fallen out the world title picture, and with new stars emerging all the time, both in Britain and beyond, Cooper's immediate prospects did not look bright, as the competition increased.

As Cooper moved into 1963 he could never have predicted how the year would end. He must have thought his career had stalled in world terms, and apart from continuing to defend his two titles against a dwindling number of legitimate contenders, only the European option held any tangible interest. The boxing public were focussed on Brian Curvis at welterweight, Terry Downes and Dave Charnley, while a huge amount of publicity was being generated around the 'Blonde Bomber' from West Ham, Billy Walker.

Henry continued training once his elbow recovered and the postponed defence against Richardson duly arrived. The fight was on 26 March at Wembley. This time the Cooper camp changed location, and took themselves to the Fellowship Inn at Catford, while Richardson, like Erskine before him, based himself once more at the Thomas a' Becket.

It's always been a bit of a shame for Henry's devoted brother, George. While Henry's career flourished and led to great success, George, we should remember, was also taking part in his own contests and doing reasonably well. He was always with Henry in training camps, often providing the sparring, and occasionally acting as a corner man, but he seemed to live in Henry's shadow. Henry would claim in later years that George was much better than his patchy record suggested. Henry believed he'd have won a lot more fights but for severely damaging his right hand not long after he turned professional, and also having the family vulnerability to cuts around the eyebrows. During the training camp for the Richardson fight, George had remarkable success in a fight he'd taken against one of the rising stars of the division, Johnny Prescott. On 12 March George travelled into Prescott's own backyard of Birmingham, and knocked him out in the second round, handing the prospect his first defeat. This must have been a valuable boost to Henry.

Amazingly, after almost nine years as a professional, and having taken part in forty six fights, this would be Richardson's first and last fight for the British title. He'd recently been European champion and earned a reputed £30,000 (over £600,000 today) for defending that crown against Johansson in Sweden. He'd been one of the quartet of young heavyweights in 1955 who'd been the subject of large

Henry Cooper: Cut Eyes and Left Hooks

bets on which one would be first to win the British title. That accolade went to Erskine, who was followed by London and then Cooper. Why Richardson had never even fought for the domestic honour up until this point is puzzling.

The fight itself was very untidy, but highly charged. Richardson's tactics seemed geared to throwing a couple of jabs to get close to Cooper, and then quite simply head butting him! This worked for the Welshman in the first round because he cut Henry over both eyes. The next couple of rounds followed the same pattern and the fight erupted at the end of the third when Richardson punched Cooper after the bell. Henry tore after Richardson and the referee and seconds had to separate them. The fourth round was more settled with Cooper getting the better of the exchanges, but the ending in the next round was unexpected. After a brief flurry of blows in a corner, Richardson dropped his guard to protect his body and Henry threw over a vicious left hook which exploded on the exposed chin and the challenger crashed to the canvas, down and out. Not only was he the loser, but sadly he never fought again, his career ending on a low note.

CHAPTER 8

The Famous Left Hook

Cassius Clay was well known in boxing circles in both America and Britain, but he hadn't up until now become a household name. Non boxing fans might have been aware of his gold medal victory at the 1960 Rome Olympics, but they would in all probability have heard little since.

The boxing pundits warmed to him because he was something new, and different. He made them smile with his antics and it was easy to like him. He appeared occasionally on the sports pages of the national newspapers in Britain with his outrageous predictions on which round he'd stop his opponents, made all the more interesting when they were proved accurate.

At around 6' 3" and weighing in the region of fourteen and a half stones he met the physical requirements of the heavyweight division, but what was bringing him notice was his speed. Clay was light on his feet being able to dance around the ring almost non-stop, not what was traditionally expected from the big lads. His greatest attribute however was the dazzling speed and timing of his punches, thrown in combinations of three or four at a time. For a twenty one year old he was exceptional.

His career was progressing sensibly. Each time he stepped into the ring the opponent was an improvement from the last occasion. As time moved on the names of those he was beating were becoming more recognisable. Alonzo Johnson – points win, Alex Miteff – TKO, Willi Besmanoff –TKO, Alejandro Lavorante –KO, Archie Moore – TKO, and Doug Jones- points win. This last fight was the one which caused some doubt about his potential. Jones was a top ten fighter and Clay predicted a fourth round knockout. Not only did his prediction fail, but there were many at ringside who felt Jones should actually have been given the decision. Clay's victory was overshadowed with booing from the New York crowd. Two judges had given the fight to Clay by a single round.

Henry Cooper: Cut Eyes and Left Hooks

Clay, with that win, was raised to the position of number three contender to Liston's crown, just behind Patterson and Johansson. Cooper, thanks to his win over Richardson, had slipped back in at number ten. Even before the Cooper/Richardson contest, the British press had already been speculating on the winner taking on Clay, in London during the summer. This suggests there must have been ongoing discussions between the group who controlled Clay and either Jack Solomons or Jim Wicks, who in turn had been leaking the discussions to certain journalists. There had been no prior suggestion that Clay's team were considering taking their man out of America, indeed a review of his fights until then showed a clear pattern of picking off higher ranked American based opposition in their quest for a title shot. If visiting Europe had been an option then the obvious target would have been Johansson.

In the middle of April Solomons caused real excitement amongst the hard bitten boxing establishment when he announced that Henry would fight Clay in the open air at Wembley Stadium on 18 June. The ageing promoter must have thought the world was against him, when new promoter Mike Barrett complained to the Boxing Board that he had a tournament arranged for the Albert Hall seven days beforehand, and in those days there had to be at least fourteen days between top level promotions. Solomons dug in his heels and told them that due to important race meetings and the availability of Wembley no other date was suitable. A special Board meeting was arranged to allow for a decision to be reached, and thankfully they endorsed the Wembley date.

The build up could now begin in earnest. The national press were even featuring Clay on their centre pages. TV and radio news programmes were discussing the fight which was still weeks away. Before Clay had even arrived on these shores all the more expensive tickets had been sold. Solomons was predicting an attendance of around 55,000 and Clay was fast becoming a media sensation.

Meanwhile Henry had quietly set up shop again at the Fellowship Inn where large numbers of local well wishers were turning up daily to the pub's converted ballroom, many of whom were known personally to the Coopers. Boxes would be handed round to the spectators inviting donations for local charities and Henry was building towards peak fitness. Through Wicks's contacts in America, he'd managed to bring over Alonzo Johnson as the main sparring partner having been advised that he closely resembled Clay's fighting style. Indeed Johnson had lost on points to Clay in his hometown of Louisville, a verdict he disputed. As the fight got nearer interested observers noticed that old foe, Joe Erskine, had also been brought in to spar a few rounds with Cooper.

Three weeks before the contest, it seemed that every member of the British media machine had converged at London Airport to welcome Clay after his twenty four hour plane journey from Kentucky. As a precursor to the visitor's willingness to garner any, and all publicity opportunities, within hours of his arrival he'd been wined and dined at Isow's restaurant in Soho along with both Cooper brothers at an organised media launch. At one point Clay believed that jet lag was playing with his mind when he noticed 'two' Henry Coopers sitting at opposite sides of the venue! Of course one was his twin brother, George.

Clay based himself at the Territorial Army, Parachute Regiment gym in Wood Lane, at the White City. His training sessions were open to the public and Clay, being the ultimate showman, revelled in all the attention. His early morning runs were conducted in Pall Mall with the innuendo that he was there to visit the Queen. Clay sparred with his brother Rudolph, and Jimmy Ellis, a fellow boxer from Louisville, who at that time competed as a middleweight.

The interest in Clay, and the fight, grew daily. Workmen in the collieries and factories were arguing over the outcome, as were women in the shops and at the school gates. Along with this interest came a polarisation of opinion on Clay. On the one hand, many thousands enjoyed his behaviour, laughed at his comments, and thought he was a refreshing change from the norm. But there was an equal, if not greater number, who hoped to see Cooper shut his big mouth. They saw Clay as arrogant and boastful.

There was, in that post war era, a distinctive British culture which applauded, modesty, respect and consideration for others. Sporting stars were expected to abide by this norm, praising their opponents, and playing down their own achievements, or better still, saying nothing. When Clay was constantly predicting he'd let Cooper survive to the fifth round 'if he behaved himself' and stating that 'Liston, Patterson, Johansson were tramps, cripples and bums', people cringed.

Quite how Clay managed to stay focussed on the fight defies logic. As well as attending a boxing show in Nottingham, he made an appearance at the Derby, and could be seen jogging around Hyde Park, usually followed by out of breath photographers.

Somehow, in those days before world sanctioning organisations existed, it'd become accepted that this ten round contest was to be a final eliminator for the world title. The more informed, specialist boxing journalists questioned that perception. With it being universally accepted that Liston would once again destroy Patterson in their return bout, they could not comprehend how either Cooper or Clay would possibly present a worthwhile challenge to the champion? Wicks had made it abundantly clear Cooper would never fight Liston, but the thought of Clay, should he win, taking on Liston was seen as simply out of the question.

The twenty one year old repeatedly declared he was the 'real champ' and this was the point where boxing experts drew the line between his humorous antics and downright stupidity. For them the thought of anyone promoting a contest between him and Liston was seen as virtually an act of criminality! Liston was widely thought of as being simply unbeatable. His brooding personality, his criminal background and his destructive power inside a boxing ring led many to believe the only heavyweight champion in history who could have stood a chance against him was Joe Louis. In actual fact nobody believed even Clay's managers would ever agree to a fight with Liston and that the young man's proclamations were made purely to gain publicity.

The weigh in was held at the London Palladium, which suited Clay – he wandered off behind the stage and found a cardboard crown among the props. That was all he needed, as he now strode around claiming he was the 'King of England'. He weighed fourteen stones, eleven pounds.

Years later Cooper revealed he'd trained so hard that as the fight approached he was weighing nearer the light heavyweight limit of twelve stones seven pounds. Before his entourage got to the Palladium, Wicks placed lead weights into the soles of Cooper's boxing boots. In addition, Henry carried another small weight in his right hand as he stepped onto the scales. His official weight was recorded as thirteen stones three and a half pounds, but he was probably half a stone lighter.

Clay was the undoubted favourite, hardly anyone of note predicted a Cooper win. Nevertheless that was certainly not how Henry and the rest of his team viewed matters. They'd been preparing to counteract Clay's obvious hand speed by moving forward to create angles which they hoped would force Clay into the corners of the ring. They also knew from Johnson, and TV films, that Clay liked to keep his hands low, particularly his right. Henry was confident that his tactics would allow him to pin Clay down in a corner and allow him to land the 'hammer'. Cooper knew from past experiences that if he could land cleanly with that punch there were very few boxers who could survive for long.

On a night of pouring rain, the Wembley crowd waited with great expectation for both men to come to the ring. The spotlights followed them from opposite ends of the stadium, and when Cooper reached the ring a huge roar erupted, while sporadic booing met his opponent, who was again wearing the cardboard crown. The night would live long in the memory, and become one of those legendary British sporting occasions, up there alongside England's World Cup victory.

The first round was a shock for all concerned, not least, to Clay. Henry stormed from his corner and went on the offensive throwing huge left hooks. Clay took several, and quickly realised that he'd a battle on his hands. Midway through the round his nose was bleeding and such was the intensity of the Cooper attacks that Clay resorted to complaining to the referee. It made no difference, with the crowd on its feet, Henry continued to press forward with considerable success and definitely won the round. Everyone watching live, and listening at home, must have begun to believe that an upset was on the cards.

In the next round Clay went on the offensive and began landing cleanly with long left jabs, one of which opened a slight cut over Cooper's left eye. However, this early show of aggression faded allowing Cooper to return fire and a solid right cross jolted Clay. This was a more even round which could have been scored either way. The third round saw the fight swing away from Henry as a result of the cut worsening, to the extent that even those at the back of the arena could see the damage. Cooper dabbed the blood away and swung the left hook in desperation, as Clay, anticipating the end may be in sight, casually jabbed towards the cut eye, dropping his hands and skipping out of range.

Danny Holland worked his magic on the cut and Cooper came out for the fourth round a little calmer. Clay seemed content to keep on the move, circling away from danger, and firing out the occasional lefts and rights endeavouring to further damage the bleeding eyebrow. As the clocked ran down to end the round Henry landed the punch that would change his life.

Henry Cooper: Cut Eyes and Left Hooks

Clay stopped moving momentarily and with his hands at his waist the 'hammer' landed with full force on the exposed jaw. The favourite was thrown backwards and collapsed onto the bottom ropes, down for the first time in his career. It was a massive punch, one that had stopped several of Henry's opponents in the past. But Clay was fit, young, and proud. Within a few seconds he was on his feet just as the bell rang. He walked to his corner quite steadily, but it was when he was forced to sit on his stool everyone realised the condition he was in. His eyes were spinning in his head, and not realising what had happened, he tried to get to his feet, before being pushed back down by Angelo Dundee, his experienced trainer. Smelling salts, illegal at the time, were pushed under his nose in an effort to bring him to his senses. Dundee, trying to buy time, hacked away at a partial tear in one of Clay's gloves hoping the next round would be delayed until a replacement was found. It didn't work, although for many years people estimated that an extra half a minute respite had been gained.

A now recovered, but badly shaken, Clay, came out for the next round, and with his first punch landed cleanly and forcibly on Cooper's left eye. A second similar punch connected, and Henry's eyebrow opened like a tomato thrown from ten storey building. Before a minute had elapsed referee Tommy Little stepped in and stopped the contest, awarding Clay the victory.

The actual result has been conveniently minimised over time, and the perennial image is of the future Muhammad Ali, probably the 'Greatest' boxer of all time, lying on the canvas supported by the bottom ropes, with Henry standing over him. Cooper had shown in the few rounds the fight lasted that he could compete at the highest level. He'd proved that 'Henry's hammer' was capable of inflicting serious damage on the very best heavyweights the world had to offer, and following on from the disaster against Folley, demonstrated he did indeed belong at the top end of his division.

Britain was proud of Cooper's effort and never forgot it. That one punch lifted Henry from being a popular, reasonably well known boxer, to a national treasure, a 'superstar' before that word was actually invented. It brought Cooper's humility, decency and approachability to the knowledge of the entire country, and ensured he was one of Britain's favourite sports personalities.

Of course, Cooper's future status as a British icon, in a perverse way, was not limited to him alone. It owed a considerable amount to the man who beat him,

Cassius Clay, later, Muhammad Ali. He would go on to do the unthinkable and beat the 'unbeatable', Sonny Liston. He became a political rallying symbol for 'black' Americans. He'd regain the world title, again beating another 'unbeatable' foe in the shape of George Foreman, and engage in arguably the most brutal fight in heavyweight history when he stopped Joe Frazier in the 'Thriller in Manila'. He carried the torch to open the Olympic Games, and became friends with Presidents.

Cooper and Clay would remain friends for the rest of their lives. Even in Clay's darkest moments while suffering from Parkinson's Syndrome, he would always make some signal to those watching when he met Cooper that he remembered the left hook. He would often jokingly remark that the punch even 'shook up my family in Africa' but he wasn't joking when he claimed it was hardest punch he ever took!

Eight months after the fight, and now known temporarily as Muhammad X, he 'shook up the world' when Liston was forced to retire at the end of the sixth round citing a shoulder injury. The truth was that Muhammad was dancing rings round him, punching him at will, and Liston couldn't lay a glove on him. He retired out of frustration and in the knowledge that if he continued he'd face further humiliation by the 'young upstart'. What did the future hold for Cooper though?

In April, Brian London had effectively ended the career of Ingemar Johansson. Although the Swede won the decision he was hanging on for dear life at the end and this probably made him realise the time had come to hang up the gloves. Technically, Cooper had to wait until the European Boxing Union declared the title vacant, but Jim Wicks was hopeful he'd be nominated to fight for it. At the same time, with Johansson gone, Henry was elevated to number five in the world. Some journalists suggested immediately after the Clay fight that Henry was considering retirement probably due to the money he'd earned, but his pre-fight suggestion never came to fruition.

In July of 1963, Sonny Liston, as expected, in the return bout, battered Patterson to defeat in one hundred and thirty seconds, and a British promotional tour was arranged for him shortly thereafter. Brian London, fresh from his close battle with Johansson, was back in favour and clambering for another match with Cooper. There was more fighting outside the ropes than in, though. A new Blackpool promoter, Lawrie Lewis, was conducting negotiations with Jim Wicks via the Boxing News trade paper. Lewis wanted to put on a fight with Cooper at a disused aircraft hanger near Blackpool, but Wicks insisted no firm offer had been made to him despite newspaper articles to the contrary. Henry's manager said he was waiting on an announcement from the European Boxing Union regarding their now vacant title. Wicks felt that they might instruct the German, Karl Mildenberger, to fight an eliminator with Santi Amonte from Italy, with the winner to face Henry. Wicks also claimed he was in discussions with Patterson's people for a fight either in Britain or Sweden.

As it turned out it was Joe Erskine, after four straight wins, who met Mildenberger in Germany. The European title was not involved, and any hopes Erskine had of jumping the queue were dashed when he lost on points. As the excitement of the Cooper/Clay contest began to fade the heavyweight focus was on the rising stars, Billy Walker and Johnny Prescott. In September the 'Blond Bomber' stopped Prescott in the last round, but two months later at a packed out Wembley, Prescott returned the favour taking the decision on points.

With the year running down to a conclusion the Boxing Board nominated London as the official challenger to Cooper for the British title and Solomons immediately tabled an offer to stage the fight. The London camp refused the terms and the Board put the contest out to purse bids. Harry Levene won this with an offer of £12,000, and the fight was scheduled for 24 February in Manchester. At the same time the European Boxing Union sanctioned the match for their championship as well. But nothing ever seems to run smoothly in professional boxing. Jim Wicks wrote to the Board and claimed that Henry was contracted to fight American Jefferson Davis in Leicester AND Floyd Patterson in Sweden before April, meaning the February date was unsuitable. Rumours began to emerge from the Board that if Cooper didn't agree to the fight within a week he'd be stripped of his British title.

CHAPTER 9

A Second Lonsdale Belt

IN ANY OTHER CIRCUMSTANCES, COOPER'S DEFENCE OF HIS BRITISH AND EMPIRE titles against Brian London on 24 February, a fight which also included the vacant European crown, would have been a significant occasion, at least in this country. After all, this was only the second time all three heavyweight titles had been on the line in a British ring, and the first since 1949, when Bruce Woodcock defeated the popular Freddie Mills.

Disappointingly for all concerned the contest took second billing to a now legendary event occurring across the Atlantic the following night. That was when Cassius Clay stunned the boxing establishment, being a 7-1 underdog, and stopped the 'unbeatable' Sonny Liston.

Not that it caused any financial loss for Harry Levene, Cooper or London. The King's Hall in Manchester was sold out weeks in advance with the Northern crowd hopeful that London, from nearby Blackpool, could upset the champion. It was not to be, however. Henry demonstrated he'd learned the art of pacing himself for a fifteen round fight, which he totally dominated with his left hand. He jabbed, hooked and uppercut London at will and when the bustling challenger got too close Cooper simply tied him up allowing him no room to move. Such was Cooper's superiority that at various stages during the 'battle' the fans broke into choruses of boos and slow handclapping, disappointed that the outcome was a foregone conclusion. Nevertheless, Henry secured his second Lonsdale belt along with a badly damaged left mitt, which may well have been broken on the brave London's head.

Injuring the hand was not a coincidence, indeed the background leading up to the damage almost caused the fight to be cancelled on the night. Apparently unknown to the Cooper team, the Boxing Board had recently altered their rules regarding the length of bandaging allowed to protect the boxer's hands. When the Board official presented the bandages to Danny Holland in the dressing room,

Henry Cooper: Cut Eyes and Left Hooks

Henry's trainer remarked that they didn't seem long enough for each hand. There was incredulity when the same official announced that the bandage supplied was for 'both' hands. Jim Wicks blew a gasket and demanded the President of the Board or his Deputy attend the dressing room to sort matters out. Word came back from ringside that those particular officials were not in charge of that evening's promotion. Knowing that the radio coverage of the fight was due to start soon, Wicks sent Henry's brother George to promoter Harry Levene to advise him that if he didn't organise a suitable compromise with the bandages he could kiss goodbye to the contest being aired live on the radio. Levene, realising that his BBC Radio fee was in jeopardy, quickly convinced the Board President to intervene. Amazingly the Board official delegated to the Cooper dressing room had only supplied bandages for one hand, and not two, although they still were shorter than before and obviously offered less protection than usual. It was a close call, because Wicks would certainly have called the fight off.

This new rule about the length of bandaging was a concern for Cooper. The existing damage to his hands was going to increase as a result. A reliable source has now confirmed how Wicks overcame the problem. Routinely, prior to a contest starting, a Board official would enter the dressing room and supervise the bandaging of a boxer's hands. Thereafter he'd place the Board's official stamp on the bandages and depart. In those days for championship contests the gloves were distributed in the ring and the official doing this could check the stamp on the bandages before the gloves were put on. Wicks had managed to purloin an official Board stamp from somewhere. After the London fight, in future contests, Wicks would wait until the Board official had left the dressing room and place additional bandaging on Cooper's hands and use his own stamp to authenticate them.

As Cooper's hand was recovering, boxing politics again reared its ugly head. With the European title now in the bag, Jim Wicks soon realised he was expected to comply with the decisions of the EBU. They wanted to keep their titles moving along and ordered Cooper to defend against the German, Karl Mildenberger. Henry enjoyed having his titles but he also liked being paid what he thought he was due when he entered the ring. His last few fights attracted purses of around £20,000 each. With the main contenders for the European heavyweight title being German, neither Solomons nor Levene would contemplate promoting a contest with someone from that country, while the second World War was still fresh in their memories. This left the door open to German and Italian promoters, who were only prepared to offer the champion around £5,000 for defending his crown. To add to the problem the British Boxing Board announced in April that they'd resigned from the EBU. This left the Cooper team with another major problem –nobody from Britain could represent their interests, as exemplified in May at the EBU congress. The EBU decided Cooper's defence against Mildenberger must take place in Germany declaring this was the only option considering Britain was no longer a member. Their logic was understandable, so too was the stipulated date of 27 July for the contest to take place.

Meanwhile Cooper's standing in terms of the world title was laid out very clearly in unusual circumstances. General Melvin Krulewitch, who was Chairman of the New York State Athletic Commission, invited the boxing press to a cocktail party at London's Cafe Royal. When asked about the world heavyweight picture he announced that his Commission had arranged an elimination process to clarify who should challenge Clay/Ali for the title. Floyd Patterson would face Eddie Machen and Cleveland Williams would meet Ernie Terrell with the winners to fight each other. He added that Doug Jones had removed himself from this scenario because he considered himself to be the legitimate number one contender. Surprisingly, given his location, the General was non-committal on where Cooper was placed!

At the end of July, with Henry having only one fight in the last thirteen months, Jim Wicks went public and explained what had been happening in the background. After allowing for Cooper's hand to recover following the London fight, Wicks was initially in discussions with Swedish promoter Eddie Ahlquist about a fight with Patterson in Stockholm. This floundered probably due to Wicks's demand for an equal share of the purse, arguing that Patterson no longer held a title. Simultaneously Wicks had refused a bid from a German promoter for Henry to defend in Germany against Mildenberger, but when a much higher bid was made by another promoter, Ferry Ohrtmann, Wicks relented and the bout was scheduled for Berlin on 5 September. Cooper's purse had risen to £9,000. Not what he wanted, but he was faced with little choice, and time was marching on.

Ohrtmann pressed on with arrangements for the open air fight, pricing ringside tickets higher than ever before for a fight in that country. Mildenberger's manager tried, but failed, to have British sparring partners sent over. Meanwhile Cooper set up camp again at the Fellowship Inn. With everything in place the contest was firstly postponed, then cancelled, and the reasons are left open to speculation.

The Boxing News reported that the day before the Cooper squad were about to fly to Germany Wicks advised them that Cooper had injured his hand, and suspecting a fracture, an x-ray was being arranged. On the same day Wicks sent a telegram to Ed Lassman, President of the World Boxing Association, offering Cooper as a replacement for Sonny Liston who'd just been banned by them from fighting Clay/Ali. Wicks also told Lassman he'd be demanding a £50,000 purse. Years later Henry would say that he'd injured his ELBOW in training and on the advice of experts was told to rest for a couple of weeks. The promoter and EBU officials travelled over to view x-rays, and made the decision to postpone the fight for a fortnight. Cooper said this proposal was totally unacceptable because it would mean he'd be going into a contest in less than peak condition. The Boxing News, a week later, indicated the fight was postponed until the middle of October, but this date never materialised and the EBU stripped Cooper of their title.

Where does the truth lie? Wicks didn't want to go to Germany in the first place, still bitter at the withholding of Cooper's purse all those years previously, and he was unhappy with the money on offer. As the fight approached, the WBA, supported by the British Boxing Board of Control, banned Liston from fighting Clay/Ali leaving him without an opponent for his title defence, with a date and venue already arranged. Moreover, the trade paper had been told by Wicks that the Mildenberger fight was off because of damage to Cooper's HAND, but Henry himself later told the authors of two books that he'd seen two named specialists regarding his troublesome ELBOW, not his fist. It's pure speculation now of course but it seems probable that Henry was carrying some sort of problem and when the possibility arose for a challenge to Clay/Ali for the world title, Wicks grabbed the opportunity to cancel the Mildenberger fight by exaggerating a pre-existing injury. The old manager was a shrewd operator, but the scheming can sometimes backfire. The prospect of a Clay/Ali fight disappeared, and with nothing else on the horizon, Cooper had lost out on a £9,000 pay day, as well as losing his European title.

While Henry's injuries were healing, brother George was involved in a TV bout with Chip Johnson, losing by knockout in the third round, and he announced his retirement immediately afterwards. Also bringing the curtain down around the same time was old foe Joe Erskine who retired following a points defeat by the 'Blonde Bomber' Billy Walker. Walker's brother, George, who was also his manager, had began telling anyone who'd listen that if he beat Erskine his next fight would be against Henry for his titles. That fight didn't happen just as quickly as George Walker hoped, but it did emphasize that Henry was now being challenged by a second generation of British heavyweights.

To demonstrate just how dry the Cooper well had become, Wicks accepted a fight at short notice, two weeks to be exact, against a fairly mediocre American, Roger Rischer. New promoter Mike Barrett had practically sold out the Albert Hall on 16 November for a fight between the hugely popular Dave Charnley and Valerio Nunez only for the 'Dartford Destroyer' to pull out nursing an illness. The only available boxer who could save the show was Henry.

Californian Rischer had been knocked out by Archie Moore and Cleveland Williams, and lost on points to both Folley and Machen. To be fair, Rischer had won his last four fights against reasonable opposition, a fact which should, perhaps, have alerted Wicks to the danger. What can't be ignored was the fact that ten months after this fight with Cooper, Rischer was knocked out by Brian London in fifty seconds!

Henry has gone down on record as saying this was one of his worst ever performances and a fight he just wanted to forget. Journalists at ringside struggled to find enough action form the ten rounds to compile a half decent report. For the first three rounds, Rischer leaned away from Cooper's left hand and when he got close enough the American tied him up until the referee struggled to separate them. Henry should have been experienced enough, and sharp enough, to overcome these tactics, but on the night he couldn't. The large Albert Hall crowd grew restless, and the booing and slow handclapping started. Still Henry couldn't motivate himself. Even the referee entered proceedings warning Rischer that he needed to do more. The eighth round probably decided the contest in Rischer's favour. What was described as a 'slap' to Cooper's groin caused him to briefly slip to the canvas, and on rising, much to the surprise of the crowd, a similar blow put Henry down again. Afterwards, Cooper, ever the realist, offered no excuses and readily admitted he had an off night.

Henry Cooper: Cut Eyes and Left Hooks

From the 'high' of 1963, when the famous left hook which floored Clay catapulted Cooper onto a completely different level in the public conscience, poor negotiations brought him back to earth with an almighty thump. After injuring his hand on London's head, he was pulled out of a title fight in Germany costing him £9,000 and eventually his European crown; was ignored as a potential challenger for the world title; and to round off a disastrous period, his defeat from Rischer kicked him out of the world top ten rankings. These events, including possibly the retirement of his best friend and brother, George, must have brought Henry to a new low.

In later life Henry talked openly about his relationship with Wicks. Apart from their first contract, limited to a three year period, they had what could be described as a 'gentleman's agreement'. Cooper trusted Wicks with all monetary and contractual matters in terms of his boxing career and it worked well for them. The close observer couldn't fail to notice that Wicks had a controlling influence on Cooper, although to be fair to the manager, everyone from that era, who is still around, will say without any doubt that it was virtually a 'father and son' relationship. Nevertheless Wicks was a former bookmaker, and well known gambler, and it's the nature of gamblers to take risks. The circumstances in the latter part of 1964 may point to Wicks having gambled and lost on this occasion in terms of Cooper's career. These were rare mistakes though.

Chapter 10

Successful Year Ends in Failure

As 1965 began Jim Wicks was once again negotiating behind the scenes. He'd had a meeting in London with black civil rights leader Malcolm X who seemed to think he was in control of Clay/Ali's boxing career. Wicks wasn't falling for that idea and passed him on to Harry Levene. At the same time Canadian George Chuvalo, who'd moved up to number five in the world rankings, was angling at a challenge to Cooper's Empire title. The Canadian's promoter offered Wicks £8,000 to bring Cooper to Toronto, and was told politely he was way off the mark!

Following the loss at the end of 1964 Wicks knew he had to get Cooper fighting again very quickly. On 12 January, back at the scene of the Rischer defeat, the Albert Hall, he faced another American, Dick Wipperman. The New York State boxer was a reasonable opponent. He'd twenty six wins, four defeats and a draw from thirty one fights. He'd been stopped only once. His last fight was a points loss to rising Argentinian fighter, Oscar Bonavena, a good performance considering how Bonavena's career would progress.

Wipperman was over a stone heavier than Cooper, and proved to be what could be termed 'live' opposition. The American was light on his feet for a big man and his left jab caused Henry problems. In a bad tempered third round the old Cooper worry, a cut eye, re-emerged. In the fifth round a strong right hand punch from Wipperman increased the damage and there were real fears of another, possibly fatal, defeat. However, the trusted left hand 'hammer' came to the rescue. It landed flush and Wipperman was knocked down and into 'cloud cuckoo land'. He bravely struggled to his feet and another thunderous left hook floored him. On rising again Wipperman was clearly seen to be disoriented, inviting the referee to quickly step in to end the fight, much to the delighted cheers of the pro Cooper crowd.

Wicks knew from past experience it was important to keep Cooper fighting regularly for him to be most effective. Three months later, in Wolverhampton,

Henry Cooper: Cut Eyes and Left Hooks

Cooper faced his third American opponent in a row, Chip Johnson, with the traditional Cooper family vengeance in mind. In November Johnson had ended the career of his brother George with a third round stoppage, and it can be supposed that the Floridian just saw that win as part and parcel of his job. Not for Henry though. The usually mild mannered Cooper always took it personal when he saw his brother beaten up. Coming in slightly heavier than usual at 13st 11lb, Cooper knocked out Johnson thirty seconds before the end of the first round. The punch? A left hook, of course!

The first generation of top level British heavyweights who grew up with Cooper, which included Richardson and Erskine, were almost gone. Only brave and determined Brian London was left, and Henry had beaten him three times. The new kids on the block, a second generation, were now making significant progress. Johnny Prescott earned the right to be the next challenger for Henry's title by beating both Billy Walker, and more recently, Brian London. Walker himself, a huge star and money making machine at the time, was also on track for a title fight, but in March was outpointed by the old warhorse, London, delaying his chances.

Since his defeat of London the previous August, Prescott had hardly covered himself in glory however. He'd drawn with Cooper victim, Chip Johnson, been disqualified against Bill Nielsen and stopped in four rounds by Hubert Hilton. In 1963 Henry's twin, George, had knocked him out and only a year previously the ageing Joe Erskine beat him on points. Prescott's nickname was 'playboy' which perhaps explains his erratic form. He was, nevertheless, very popular in the Midlands, and, when fit, could be a really good fighter.

Despite all the criticism of Prescott's 'playboy' lifestyle, he perhaps deserved a bit of fun in his life. His father had been killed at Dunkirk, his mother killed in an air raid, and he'd been brought up in an orphanage until he was thirteen. His professional career had kicked off in promising fashion. In the first sixteen months he'd taken part in an incredible twenty contests, winning eighteen, ten by knockout, with two draws. His first loss was the one to George Cooper.

A report exists which once again showed that Henry did, very occasionally, have a nasty streak, similar in nature to incidents during his previous encounters with Joe Erskine and Brian London. A few years before his title challenge, Prescott had been invited down to the Thomas a' Becket to spar with Cooper. For some unknown reason Henry 'went to town' on him, forcing those present to step in and bring the 'training' session to an abrupt halt. This is rare in professional boxing, especially when you have an experienced champion sparring with a young hopeful. Londoners of the time would describe what Henry did as 'taking a liberty'. Perhaps the young Prescott had been over confident and was starting to believe his own publicity causing Henry to put him in his place?

The championship bout was a joint promotion between Jack Solomons and Midlander Alex Griffiths, and scheduled for 15 June, outdoors at the home of Birmingham City football club. As is always the danger with these arrangements in a country like Britain the rain came down causing the event to be postponed for a couple of days.

Unknown to anyone at the time, Wicks was already in serious discussions with Ali's people about a world title fight. Victories over Wipperman and Johnson, added to a previous promise made to Wicks, made a title fight a real possibility. Cooper was aware of these discussions and approached the Prescott fight in the knowledge that he had to win at all costs.

Prescott's manager, George Biddles, brought in the old welterweight champion, Jack Hood, to assist with his efforts to prevent Cooper dominating the fight and for the first few rounds Prescott had some success. Henry was unable to land cleanly because Prescott kept close and moved well. Gradually though, Cooper began to land the occasional hook and powerful body shots when Prescott tried to tie him up. These were having an effect and the local fighter began to show signs of fatigue. The breakthrough for Cooper came in the eighth round when a partially blocked short left hook, followed by solid punch to the unguarded stomach dropped Prescott onto both knees. He wasn't badly hurt and got to his feet quickly, but the writing was on the wall. In the tenth round a further two short left hooks accounted for two more brief counts, and at the end of this round Prescott's manager had seen enough, calling the referee over to offer his retirement. The unsympathetic Birmingham crowd booed their own man, but he'd done his best and was simply outclassed. Physically Cooper had looked in tip top condition and boxed superbly. The fight was watched by 18,000 spectators.

While one of George Biddles's heavyweight hopes had been thwarted, he'd another potential challenger up his sleeve in the shape of awkward southpaw, Jack Bodell.

Henry Cooper: Cut Eyes and Left Hooks

The Derbyshire man had notched up twenty eight wins from thirty three fights, nineteen of those wins coming inside the distance, and he was moving into contention to challenge for Henry's British crown. Billy Walker however was losing further ground having lost to London, followed by a draw in Italy with Eduardo Corletti, a fight watched live in San Remo by Cooper while on holiday visiting his wife's family. London too, was again being touted as Henry's next challenger, a prospect that didn't impress many people.

The possibility of a world title challenge withered when Ali decided to defend against former champion, Floyd Patterson. Wicks was determined however to keep Henry active given his recent run of success. Harry Levene arranged a promotion at Wembley for 19 October and put together a bill featuring three heavyweight fights. Appearing in fights alongside Cooper would be the 'Golden Boy' Billy Walker and Johnny Prescott. Levene might have ended up being satisfied with his profits from the event, but British boxing suffered two significant blows.

Henry's opponent was yet another American, Amos Johnson, who was just outside the world's top ten rankings. A quick look at his record would have shown Wicks that he seemed the ideal foe. From twenty four fights he'd won nineteen with only nine stoppages, suggesting he wasn't a lethal puncher. Significantly, amongst his three defeats, was a first round knockout at the hands of former Cooper victim, Chip Johnson. A year previous though, Amos had travelled to Germany and secured a draw with Mildenberger which given the quality of officiating there, would have implied that he'd actually won convincingly!

When the Cooper fight got under way he looked very fit and confident and the fans must have settled back in the hope of enjoying another convincing victory for the British champion. Johnson also appeared relaxed and unconcerned, seemingly having little regard for Henry's vaunted left hook. Towards the middle part of the round Cooper was rushed into the ropes, and a left hook from Johnson landed around the midriff causing him to sink to his knees. Referee Harry Gibbs quickly jumped in and when Cooper got to his feet he brought both boxers together and seemed to warn the American. Almost all reports of the incident at the time stated that it was a low blow which brought Henry down. However, slow motion viewing of the fight film demonstrates that the punch landed right on the waistband of Cooper's shorts. Nowadays that would've been considered a legal punch. Shortly after the fight re-commenced Johnson landed another left hook to Cooper's body and this time the punch WAS low, right into the groin area.

Once again in the sixth round, Cooper slumped to the floor from a definite low blow, with Gibbs issuing a warning to Johnson. After a rather messy contest the American got the verdict from Harry Gibbs. It was a close fight, and not as 'dirty' as many commentators at the time alleged. On reflection, it perhaps could have gone Cooper's way, there wasn't much in it. The result demonstrated once again that referee's in this country were certainly not biased towards the local fighter!

Cooper was interviewed in the dressing room by Harry Carpenter after the fight. Henry's comments summed up the man, and would bring respect from anyone who values sportsmanship. He made absolutely no excuses for the defeat and refused to be drawn into any implied criticism of Johnson. He also added that he'd prepared properly, had no injuries, but simply couldn't perform at his best on the night. Carpenter tried to push him on the retirement issue, but Henry rejected the idea. Rather embarrassingly Carpenter pointed out that the defeat would have cost Cooper his top ten position in the world rankings, and while a lesser individual may have began to get a bit defensive at that point, Henry simply shrugged his shoulders and agreed with the interviewers suggestion.

The other disappointment for Levene was the technical knockout suffered by Walker.

The final few months of each year were proving to be unpopular as far as Cooper's career was concerned. In December 1960, while beating Alex Miteff comfortably, Cooper had almost thrown it away by being flattened in the last round. Exactly a year later Zora Folley had knocked Henry out in the second round. In 1962 and 1963 Henry didn't have any fights in that period but in November 1964 he experienced a shocking loss to Riger Rischer and then came the defeat by Johnson.

The recent defeat to Johnson once again threw up an apparent weakness Henry seemed to have concerning body punches. From the first round when he was dropped by a possibly legitimate punch to the midriff Henry seemed to wince every time Johnson went to that region and this wasn't the first time this had happened. Going all the way back to the defeat from Joe Bygraves there were numerous examples of a surprising inability to cope with those sort of punches.

In the immediate aftermath of the Johnson fight, and even though Cooper had declared he wasn't considering retirement, the national press were speculating that the plan was to have him fight only twice more, in British title defences, in the hope he'd secure a third Lonsdale belt. London was top of everyone's list to be the next challenger, but the Blackpool boxer himself didn't fancy the job. Billy Walker would have been a money spinner but his loss on the same night as Cooper's defeat, to Argentinian Eduardo Corletti, diminished his standing. Strangely enough Corletti had been Henry's principal sparring partner in the lead up to the Johnson fight, and although handled easily by the British champion, he performed well enough to persuade Wicks to become his new agent in Britain.

At the beginning of November, the Boxing News version of the world rankings made interesting reading. Brian London, thanks to his recent form, was listed as the number nine contender while Henry had dropped back to twelve. The World Boxing Association, removed Ali as their champion for refusing to fight Ernie Terrell, and installed him at the top. Meanwhile the rest of the known world still recognised Ali. Also of note, given that Cooper still held the Empire title, was the fact that Canadian George Chuvalo was listed at number four, and the highest ranked European was Mildenberger. Fights against either Chuvalo or Mildenberger could have attracted a lot of attention, and wins would have raised Henry up the rankings significantly.

Regardless of the politics involved Ali did indeed defend against Patterson stopping him in the twelfth round, punishing the injured former champion mercilessly because he refused to recognise his Muslim name. The humour was starting to fade from Ali's professional life.

By the end of 1965 Henry's popularity beyond the boxing ring was further demonstrated when he was invited to lunch with the Queen at Buckingham Palace along with other well known celebrities. How much this meant to such an ordinary every day person like Cooper was made clear years later when he was able to recall every detail from the occasion for his biographer.

Chapter 11

The World Title Fight

THE YEAR THAT BECAME THE MOST IMPORTANT OF HENRY COOPER'S ENTIRE boxing career was 1966, when he finally got his chance to fight for the world title, and the opportunity was closely linked to events surrounding the champion, Muhammad Ali, as he now wanted to be known.

America was at war with Vietnam, and had to rely on conscription, or the 'draft', as it was called, to recruit sufficient soldiers. Every male over eighteen years, not in a reserved occupation, had to be physically and intellectually tested to assess their suitability. Ali easily passed the physical, but failed the intelligence test! A procedure existed for the intelligence test to be repeated under the watchful gaze of psychologists to ensure that those being tested were not deliberately failing in order to avoid the 'draft'. Ali failed the second test as well, leading to several insulting comments from the American press. Ali claimed that he struggled with reading because he'd hardly attended school as a youngster and couldn't begin to understand the questions.

In February 1966 the American government lowered the qualification score for the intelligence test, and Ali, to his horror, was placed on the 'draft' list. Under pressure from the media, and from the Nation of Islam, Ali made several anti-war statements causing a massive backlash from the public, many of whom had already lost loved ones in the conflict. A world title defence against Ernie Terrell in Chicago scheduled for March was banned by the city authority, and when a host of other cities who could have taken the event came out and also announced they wanted no part of Ali, his management group realised that, at least in the short term, he'd have to travel outwith America for future defences. This was part of the background to Henry's world title opportunity.

Prior to these events, and for the sixth time, in a career going back just over eleven years, Cooper took a fight in January, this time on a Harry Levene promotion at Olympia in London. His opponent was yet another American, Hubert Hilton.

Henry Cooper: Cut Eyes and Left Hooks

On the same bill was Wicks's Argentinian hopeful Eduardo Corletti, who was facing George Chuvalo. Chuvalo had retained his number four ranking, and it was obvious that Wicks had engineered a 'win-win' situation for Henry, providing he dealt with Hilton. If, as expected, Chuvalo was to prevail then an Empire title fight with him and Cooper would be an obvious match-up. On the other hand a victory for Corletti, given that the Argentine was being handled easily as a sparring partner by Cooper, would surely remove Chuvalo from his high status as a leading contender.

Hilton was a pretty average, but durable opponent, with thirteen wins from seventeen fights. He'd never been stopped, and until March the previous year there had been no recognisable names on his record. That was when he came to England and stopped Johnny Prescott in the fourth round. Two months later he repeated the dose, stopping Prescott's stablemate, Jack Bodell, in the sixth.

It had also now become known that Henry had suffered a broken thumb before the Johnson fight, a fact that was kept quiet at the time, and there was slight concern among the Cooper camp as to how well this injury had healed.

They needn't have worried about the thumb because Cooper destroyed Hilton without breaking sweat! From the first bell he dominated his opponent, landing cleanly with stinging jabs and soon putting him on the defensive. Midway through the next round Henry saw his chance and over came 'the hammer'. Down went Hilton, who showed his relative inexperience by rising too quickly and stumbling about like a newborn deer. The referee stepped in and waved it over, much to the annoyance of the visitor, who would have been knocked out completely if he'd been allowed to continue. It's unfathomable how Cooper could perform like this, and then struggle to defeats against the likes of Rischer and Johnson. Nevertheless, Cooper had put himself back in the world title picture, but Chuvalo was not so fortunate. He suffered a setback, losing on points to Corletti. Under normal circumstances the defeat should have sent him tumbling out the top ten. However, in the strange world of professional boxing, his next fight would be in his hometown of Toronto, against Ali, for the ultimate prize.

At the beginning of February, no one had given any thought to Chuvalo meeting Ali, because of the scheduled fight between the champ and Ernie Terrell. Jim Wicks, however, advised the press he was already working closely with Ali's people for a challenge by Cooper soon after the Terrell fight, providing of course Ali won. In the meantime Cooper was back in the ring again, less than a month later.

Wicks had forged a good relationship with Midland promoter Alex Griffiths, and Henry topped the bill at his promotion in Wolverhampton. In the opposite corner would be yet another fighter from across the Atlantic in the shape of Jefferson Davis. The old 'revenge' angle appeared once more, similar to that which existed when Cooper met Brian London, Dick Richardson and Chip Johnson. In October 1963 Davis stopped George with a badly cut eye in the seventh round, while Henry had been in his corner. For some time afterwards Henry tried to persuade Wicks to set up a match purely to allow him to settle the score.

According to all reports Davis had never been off his feet in thirty four bouts. He'd won twenty six, drawn one, and all seven losses were on points. Among those defeats were the names of Thad Spencer, Amos Johnson, Ernie Terrell and Karl Mildenberger. He was also a good two inches taller than Cooper.

Henry was back to his brilliant best. The fighter who looked jaded, and fading towards possible retirement against Rischer and Johnson, was nowhere to be seen. A series of short left hooks towards the middle of the first round had Davis holding on, and Henry just kept on hitting him with the same punch until the American collapsed to the canvas, to be counted out 'dead to the world'.

From November 1964 until this victory over Davis, a period of some fifteen months, Henry had fought seven times. If we exclude the British title defence against Prescott, the remainder were against pretty similar American opponents. It took Cooper less than nine rounds to knock out four of them, yet Rischer and Amos Johnson took him the full distance and won on points. Henry always maintained he fought better around 13st 7lb, but he was within four pounds of that ideal weight for all six contests.

It's interesting to take a look at how all these opponents fared after fighting him. Rischer lost a lopsided battle for the Californian State title to Thad Spencer and was then knocked out in a round by Brian London. Wipperman won his next five fights but a year after facing Cooper he was stopped in the fifth round by Joe Frazier. Chip Johnson lost five of his next six contests including a fifth round knockout to Prescott. Over the next two years Amos Johnson won two and lost the rest. He was knocked out in the third round by both Sonny Liston and Leotis Martin, disqualified in the seventh against Brian London and beaten on points by Oscar Bonavena. In the two years following his fight with Cooper, Hilton won four and lost five. In his next fight he lost on points to Jimmy Ellis, and had further stoppage defeats against Bonavena and Mac Foster. He certainly wasn't a poor fighter. The last on the list was Davis. He had another seven fights before calling it a day. He was knocked out in the eighth round by Folley and shortly after, took him the full distance. His last contest was a fifth round knockout at the hands of Joe Frazier.

This review shows that all those boxers were decent opponents and had fairly similar abilities. What then could be the explanation for the two defeats? It was well known that Henry was always in the gym and saw it simply as his job to keep fit. Training was certainly stepped up for championship contests, when he set up camp at bases away from home, so not being properly prepared could not be an excuse. Perhaps the only 'unexplained' defeat previously was his loss to Joe Bygraves in 1957 when a sluggish performance ended with a body shot putting him down and out. When he lost to Rischer and Johnson, Henry seemed to put it down to a 'bad day at the office'. He couldn't explain clearly how he didn't seem able to get his punches off or why his timing wasn't what it should have been. Lack of sparring can sometimes explain this, but there are no indications that this was the case. We then have to look at how focussed Henry was at the time.

With regard to the Amos Johnson fight we know that Henry had just been persuaded to open a green grocery business near his home in Wembley. It would seem that part of the potential for success in such a business rested in the idea that customers, as well as buying the product, could have a fair chance of meeting the 'owner'. In addition to actually being in the shop, Henry found himself spending more time in learning how a business operated, buying and selling, profit margins, rates, electricity etc. It's entirely possible that Cooper became distracted by this, and although physically training as hard and as often as usual, his mind might not have been fully 'on the job'? To support this theory we need only glance at his performance immediately afterwards, when perceiving his boxing future in jeopardy, put business interests to the side, concentrated on his main line of work, and got back to winning ways. There is now no known background explanation for the poor performance against Rischer, but perhaps, once again he'd been distracted in some way? In essence, it seems likely that the principal reason for these unexpected defeats was 'mental' and not 'physical'.

Jim Kirkwood

Events in America during March gave the boxing public a glimpse of the future. As no US state would sanction a fight involving Muhammad Ali, for fear of a public outcry due to his refusal to be drafted, Toronto volunteered to host his fight with Terrell. When contracts were about to be signed, Terrell rejected the money on offer, and pulled out. Very quickly, Main Bouts Incorporated, who promoted Ali, arranged for the promotion to go ahead with George Chuvalo replacing Terrell. The World Boxing Association, for whom Terrell was the champion, immediately announced they would not recognise the fight, declaring Chuvalo was not a suitable opponent. Their decision shouldn't have caused too much concern because the entire world still recognised Ali as the champ anyway! Chuvalo bravely lasted the full distance, losing widely on points.

In April, Harry Levene announced he'd secured a world title fight for Henry against Ali, to be staged in the open air at Highbury Stadium home of Arsenal football club. For the British boxing public and the sporting press, this felt like a moment when the earth moved! There hadn't been a world heavyweight title fight in Britain since 1908, and now the ever popular British champ, who three years previously had temporarily buttoned that 'Louisville Lip', would be challenging a boxer slowly emerging as one of the most well known sporting personalities in the western world! The money being discussed was huge for the time. Ali was guaranteed £100,000, Cooper half that figure, but both boxers were on additional percentages from television rights (£100,000 then is valued at £1.75 million in 2016). Jointly involved with the promotion was Jarvis Astaire's company, Viewsport, who had access to the new satellites which were able to send live film of the fight throughout the world.

Hundreds of people were on the tarmac when Ali's aircraft taxied to a stop in early May. The champion was first off wearing a black suit and bow tie, looking every bit the image many British people had seen of the black civil rights leader, Malcolm X. The scene was one expected of visiting royalty. The following day the 'great man' attended an official press reception at the Piccadilly Hotel from which both the BBC and ITV were banned due to their failure to show his recent fights. One famous quip from Ali summed up the difference in attitude from his visit three years previously, "I used to say 'I'm The Greatest' now people tell me 'I'm The Greatest'". In the evening Ali was invited to a reception organised by the Boxing Writers Club

Henry Cooper: Cut Eyes and Left Hooks

at the Cafe Royal where he was presented with a miniature boxing ring with the inscription, 'Cassius Clay, Unbeaten World Champion'.

The pre-fight excitement gripped the nation, and there were even advertisements telling people how they could get tickets to watch Ali and Cooper's training sessions. Ali trained at the TA Drill Hall, White City between one and two thirty pm while at the same time Cooper would be at the Thomas a' Becket. Bizarrely, the entire British press, and the public, still referred to the champion as Cassius Clay, and Ali himself didn't seem to take any offence.

The Cooper team based themselves at the Duchess of Edinburgh Hotel in Welling, with Henry doing a lot of his running and specialised preparations there, away from the public gaze, before moving up in the afternoons to the Thomas a' Becket. With the fight being staged in London, Henry only had to follow his normal routine which must have been seen as a distinct advantage. Of course there had to be several minor disruptions in order to help sell the fight. There was the initial meeting with Ali, a visit to the state of the art facility from where film of the fight would be relayed, and dinner with the Sports Writers Association when Henry was shown the impressive Boxing News Gold Cup he'd be awarded if he won the title.

The bookmakers had Henry as a 7-1 underdog but there was real belief in the Cooper camp that a victory was possible. Although Henry would receive the biggest purse of his career, that fact was very much at the back of his mind. He knew, from the knock down in their first fight, that if he could catch Ali, he could hurt him, so they worked on doing just that. Jim Wicks made the comment that if he could guarantee Henry's eyes could hold out he was certain his man would win. How prophetic that turned out to be. Another factor in Henry's favour was he knew he could pace himself over the fifteen rounds championship distance – he'd done it three times previously. Ali had only managed that once, in his last fight with Chuvalo. The camp knew how quick Ali was, but no one could keep that speed up for fifteen rounds. So they must have felt they had two favourable chances. Either the left hook would catch the champion cleanly early on, or as Ali slowed down, Henry might start to score points in the later rounds.

There is no doubt Ali was taking the fight seriously. Trainer Angelo Dundee placed a photograph of the Cooper knock down on the wall of their gym in Miami to remind the champion of his vulnerability. Dundee also told the press in America that Cooper had the best left hook in world boxing at the time, and of course Ali himself would have remembered how hurt he was in 1963. To emphasize his concern, Ali weighed in at the lightest he'd been for four years, and, quite amazingly, almost a stone less than he weighed for the Chuvalo defence only eight weeks beforehand. To add to what was clearly a plan by Dundee to have his man quick on his feet and out of reach of the Cooper 'hammer' was his insistence in having an extremely large twenty foot ring installed. This was so unusual that promoter Levene had to have one specially made before Ali would sign off on the fight contract.

Henry would later tell his biographer that the nerves only started to hit him when his passage to Highbury Stadium began to be blocked by the huge crowds, as his police escorted Rolls Royce carried him, George, Danny Holland and Jim Wicks to the fight. Every single family member, and close friends, were going to be there alongside 45,000 spectators and millions more listening on the radio. Viewsport were beaming live pictures to cinemas in Birmingham, Manchester, Coventry, Southampton, Glasgow, Nottingham, Leeds, Norwich, Cardiff, Leicester, Newcastle and three further locations in London.

When the fanfare started it took ten minutes for Henry to force himself through the crowds from his dressing room to the ring as the fans chanted his name. This time there were no cardboard crowns and theatrics when Ali entered the ring, it was all business. Right from the first bell Cooper showed he'd no fear of the champion and went immediately onto the offensive. The round was very even with each boxer landing only a few scoring punches. The next must have been scored, albeit marginally, to Cooper as he managed to force Ali into the corners of the huge ring. The third round was very close and could have been scored either way. The fourth and fifth rounds seemed to have been Cooper's but at that stage no one could have said with any confidence whether either fighter was streaking ahead. Certainly, the betting odds were being turned on their heads.

As Cooper once again came out in confident and aggressive mode, disaster struck. Ali threw a long left jab followed by a full force downward right cross which landed right on the upper edge of Cooper's protruding left eyebrow. The eyebrow burst open immediately and Henry knew it was a bad one. He shook his head and the blood spattered over the canvas. A dab at the eye with his left glove confirmed the worst. Cooper now had to go for a quick knockout. He launched into reckless attacks in the hope he could catch the champion, but instead of running, Ali stood his ground and caught the challenger repeatedly as he made mistake after mistake in his desperation. The referee stopped the fight to assess the injury and briefly allowed it to continue, but he must have realised it couldn't last much longer. He was giving Cooper a short window of opportunity to turn things around. It was not to be. Ali began landing cleanly and powerfully and the third man in the ring quickly brought proceedings to a close. Henry swung his fists down out of sheer frustration as Jim Wicks climbed onto the ring apron in a forlorn attempt to indicate that the cut was caused by a clash of heads. It most definitely was not!

The fight didn't reach the halfway stage, but up until the end Cooper demonstrated he was not only a worthy world title challenger but as good an opponent for Ali as anyone around at the time.

Arguments persist to this day as to whether Ali was the greatest heavyweight champion in history. The debate is complicated further by the fact that there were 'two' Ali's. The one who fought until 1967 when he was forced into retirement due the political situation he found himself in, and the older, heavier and slower version who re-emerged in 1970. With Frazier, Foreman and Norton alongside Ali, the 1970s are considered the 'golden age' for heavyweight boxing. Ali's victories over Frazier, Foreman and Norton are legendary. It has to be remembered that Frazier and Norton actually beat Ali, and Foreman pounded him in Zaire before being stopped, an exhausted wreck. In the 1960s nobody beat him. In fact hardly anyone laid a glove on him.

If the Ali of the 1960s was the better version, then Cooper's efforts in both his fights showed just how good a performer he was. Those fights confirmed that Henry was truly a world class heavyweight deserving of the accolades afforded him by the British public.

CHAPTER 12

Knocked Out by Patterson, but Third Lonsdale Belt

THE MORNING AFTER THE ALI DEFEAT HENRY PAID FOR EXPENSIVE PLASTIC surgery on his injured eyebrow, a cut reckoned to have been the worst in his career so far. While the boxing press speculated that perhaps this would have been his last fight, Henry himself had no such thoughts. On looking back, shortly after his career eventually came to an end, Henry himself felt at the time that any hope of another world title fight had gone for good. However during the remainder of the summer Wicks had other ideas and begun planning Cooper's next fight with a view to keeping him in world title contention!

Seven years previously Wicks almost secured a world title challenge to Floyd Patterson but drew out of negotiations being unsatisfied with the money on offer. That opportunity then fell to Brian London. Now in August the same Brian London had engineered a second attempt at the world championship. The tough Blackpool man often remarked that he hated boxing and only did it for the money. That became crystal clear when he succumbed rather easily to the fists of Ali in the third round of their bout at Earl's Court. However Wicks still had good relations with Patterson's people and felt that if he could arrange a fight between him and Henry, and if he could secure a win, then it would keep him in contention for a second challenge to Ali. Wicks knew Ali was being forced to defend his title outside America due to the political climate, and given the financial success of their last bout, he was confident another world title fight in London was entirely possible.

Although Jim Wicks had went on record to say he wouldn't allow Henry to fight Sonny Liston, and they were suggestions, mostly from within the Chuvalo camp, that Wicks had made similar comments about fighting the Canadian, once contracts for a fight had been finalised, Wicks was always satisfied his man would win. Unknown to Cooper, for obvious reasons, Wicks was not so confident in the lead up to the Patterson fight. The old manager had serious concerns Patterson might just have the tools to beat his man mainly due to the knowledge that Cooper's elbow damage was causing him real problems. The injury had been present for a number of years, and the camp knew that when fighting taller opponents the arm didn't cause as much pain. Patterson though was shorter than Henry by a couple of inches and Wicks lost sleep over the possibility he wouldn't be able to throw the left hook properly. Not an edifying prospect when fighting someone as lethal as the former champion.

Critics of Patterson point to his two crushing defeats by Sonny Liston and his relatively few, and less than dangerous defences, during his six year reign as world champion, only interrupted briefly by a loss to Johansson. But Patterson was a superbly coached boxer, with the ability to knock opponents out with either hand. He either launched a dangerous leaping left hook, or his punches were delivered close up, and in rapid combinations. He wasn't particularly big, standing around 6' and usually weighing around 14st but was extremely quick, usually being able to duck below the punches from bigger foes, and counter attacking at speed. He had however the punchers' weakness – a glass chin! The number of knockdowns he suffered are almost too numerous to count, but more times than not he'd struggle back to his feet and carry on.

When he fought Cooper in September 1966 it had been three years since he was dethroned, but there was no sign he'd given up the chance to win the title back. In his six fights since losing to Liston his only defeat had come to Ali, having beaten Eddie Machen and George Chuvalo on points. Indeed after this fight with Cooper he'd fight another fifteen times losing only to Jerry Quarry, in an eliminator for the world title, to Jimmy Ellis for the WBA version of the world title, and in his last fight to Ali when a badly swollen eye forced a stoppage. Notable among his other fights was a draw with Quarry and a points win over Oscar Bonavena.

Wicks's worries were well founded. When Patterson entered the ring to fight Cooper he'd been fighting for fourteen years, winning forty three of forty eight contests, with thirty two opponents failing to hear the final bell.

The fight attracted a lot of interest. There were many who thought Henry was unlucky against Ali and were keen to see him continue to box at world level. Similarly, the public were desperate to see the former world champion fight in the flesh, they'd heard so much about him for such a long period of time. Due to their demeanour outside the ring, both men were extremely popular with the sporting public and brought credit to the sport.

There was however an unsavoury chapter in the build up to the fight. Jim Wicks had engaged New Yorker, Billy Daniels, as a sparring partner for Cooper. Daniels was due to fight Billy Walker on the same night as the Patterson bout but was suddenly replaced by a German Horst Benedens. A few days after the event a Sunday newspaper broke the story that Daniels had been offered a bribe to lose to Walker. When Daniels spoke to the press he claimed he'd told Jim Wicks about the bribe. A journalist called Wicks and tape recorded their conversation. Wicks admitted what Daniels had said and had advised him to having nothing to do with it. The Walker camp who claimed to have had no knowledge of the bribe were upset that Wicks hadn't reported the situation to the Board of Control.

Cooper started the bout in confident mood and seemed to have little regard for Patterson's reputation. Henry probably edged the first two rounds, with only brief flurries coming from Patterson when he would virtually throw himself into attack in an effort to land a big left hook. Round three followed the same pattern with the crowd starting to get behind Cooper when they believed he seemed to be hurting Patterson with left hooks to the body. Towards the end of the round, just when Cooper seemed to be taking the ascendency, the American threw a swinging left uppercut which landed forcefully on the point of Henry's chin. Patterson's momentum was still carrying him forward and a further left hook and short right cross put Cooper down onto the seat of his trunks. The British champion wasn't hurt, rising easily to his feet and as the round ended he walked steadily back to his corner apparently unconcerned.

Cooper began the fourth round as if nothing had happened, and was again dictating the pace when a leaping left hook caught him on the side of the head, and he was floored once more. This time he got himself onto his knees and looked to his corner. Henry rose at the count of nine and seemed more frustrated at himself than anything else. Shortly after, he was to receive the hardest punch in his long career, and not only did he not feel it, he never even saw it coming. As he moved forward to throw a jab, Patterson launched a straight right hand missile which landed with full force on the exposed Cooper jaw. Henry dropped face first to the canvas and was counted out as he tried to push himself up. To be honest the referee could have counted to a hundred and poor Henry still wouldn't have managed to rise on his own. All the while the kind hearted Patterson was trying to lift him up and appeared embarrassed about what he'd done.

Cooper had been flattened previously by Johansson and Folley and on both occasions he'd managed to stagger to his feet, and was simply unable to continue within the allotted time. This was different, he was well and truly knocked out!

Once again it was decision time for Cooper. He remained British and Empire champion, but the number one challenger for the domestic crown was still reckoned to be Brian London who he'd beaten three times. He'd now lost two bouts in quick succession at world level. He was thirty two years old, not too advanced an age for a heavyweight by today's standards, but, his contemporaries when he started out had all been younger when they'd hung up the gloves. Joe Erskine was retired at thirty, Dick Richardson retired even younger at twenty eight, Peter Bates was twenty nine, and even Ingemar Johansson was gone by the age of thirty.

More important was his domestic situation. His wife by all accounts didn't like boxing. The first fight she saw, and her last, was the world title challenge. She saw blood flying from her husband's eyebrow as another man tried his hardest to punch the injured spot repeatedly. If that wasn't enough, four months later she would've been aware that he'd been knocked senseless. Reports suggest she encouraged Henry to retire.

Many years later Cooper himself would say that he didn't like the idea of the press advising him to throw in the towel. He wanted it to be his decision alone. He was confident he could handle any British challenger at the time and felt the current European champion, Mildenberger, posed no real worries. Being relatively fit and healthy, and a few more 'pay days' were possible, why should he not carry on? Cooper's career did continue, but not even those closest to him could have envisaged he'd still be boxing at the top of his game four and a half years later.

On 21 October 1966 a disaster occurred at the Welsh village of Aberfan in Wales which no one living at the time will ever forget. Due to heavy rain a coal tip turned into slurry, and slid downwards to cover a school, killing one hundred and sixteen children and twenty eight adults. Such was the measure of a man such as Cooper, within two weeks of the tragedy, he offered to fight anyone for free, with all proceeds going to assist the disaster fund. Not an insignificant offer given that he was attracting purses at that time of around £20,000 (valued at £350,000 in 2016). Old foe Joe Bygraves put himself forward, also offering to give up his purse, and then there was speculation that new Welsh hope, Carl Gizzi could be in the opposite corner at a promotion held in Cardiff. Sadly for all concerned 'boxing politics' scuppered Cooper's generous offer. With referee Ike Powell and matchmaker Les Roberts adding their names to the list of people wishing to be involved without recompense, there was still no one prepared to pull all the strands together to make it happen, and the charitable plan fell through.

Henry hadn't defended his British title since June 1965 and the managers of the leading contenders were urging the Board to make a decision as to who he should face. Billy Walker's manager was insisting on a direct challenge by his man without the need for an eliminator. In response, the Board deemed that Johnny Prescott should face his stablemate, Jack Bodell , with the winner to be the official challenger. Prescott pulled out, and Brian London became the replacement. London also withdrew, but Walker's manager still refused to agree to an eliminator with Bodell. In reality, as far as the London based promoters were concerned, Bodell was a clumsy and unattractive fighter who was not popular enough to attract a crowd of sufficient number to make it financially worthwhile, a situation which naturally annoyed the big Swadlincote boxer immensely.

In December the Board resolved the matter. They decided Cooper must defend against Bodell before the end of June and called for purse bids. This set George Walker, Billy's brother and manager, off in an alternative direction. He took aim at Mildenberger's European title.

The first few months of 1967 passed with Henry's name missing from all boxing discussions. Eventually an announcement was made that he would indeed fight Bodell at Wolverhampton Wanderers football ground on 13 June. Meanwhile George Walker's plan for Billy came to fruition. He first fought, and beat, an undefeated Italian, Giulio Rinaldi, a contest viewed as an unofficial eliminator for the European crown, and Harry Levene thereafter arranged for Walker to challenge Mildenberger in March at Wembley. The promotion was a huge success financially, but Walker was handled easily by the German and the fight was stopped in the eighth round. The bout also ended the apparent embargo on German boxers fighting for the top London promoters, Levene and Solomons.

Henry Cooper: Cut Eyes and Left Hooks

The unfortunate Bodell had kept in shape with a points victory over Floyd Patterson's brother, Ray, in January, and Midlands promoter Alex Griffiths, in an obvious attempt to enhance their up and coming title fight, had Cooper and Bodell fighting on the same bill in Leicester on 17 April. Originally Henry's scheduled opponent was another American, Henry Clark. However, a week before the contest Clark pulled out, followed quickly by another withdrawal this time by Jamaican, Wendell Newton. After a series of frantic phone calls, Griffiths eventually secured the services of Boston Jacobs.

Jacobs was not really at Cooper's level and a glimpse at his record would have demonstrated how desperate Griffiths must have been to keep Cooper on his promotion. Jacobs had been fighting professionally for three years and in nine bouts had lost three. The only recognisable name was Chuvalo, who'd stopped him in the third round.

Henry came in five pounds over his best fighting weight and didn't look to be in peak condition. His performance reflected this. Looking stale, the situation worsened in the third round, when a bad cut appeared over the vulnerable left eye. Wicks would later claim it resulted from a head clash, but others at ringside believed it was caused by a right hander from Jacobs. Cooper staggered the visitor in the fifth round with a vicious left hook causing him to stumble face first into the ropes but Henry was too slow in following up. In the tenth round Cooper was again seen to be bleeding from further cuts over and under the right eye. Nevertheless, he'd clearly won the fight but to some observers his performance seemed to suggest that he really was nearing the end of the road. Afterwards in the dressing room, Cooper, unusually for him, complained about the head clashes and felt the referee should have disqualified Jacobs. These comments were so untypical of Henry, and serve to illustrate how unhappy he'd been throughout the whole fight.

In those days, experienced managers would not let their fighters even begin to spar until six months had elapsed following a bad knockout. Wicks had always been very careful with Henry's health and it's likely he wouldn't have been in a boxing ring before the middle of March. Being overweight supports this claim, and that, coupled with a lack of sharpness probably due to insufficient time spent on sparring, may have been behind the poor performance.

Of course, the way Cooper had fought against Jacobs fuelled speculation, prior to Cooper's next big outing against Bodell, that he might be ready 'for the taking'. Could the younger man be about to end the long reign of the champion?

The boxing press had been harsh in their summation of the challenger, and on reflection there might have been more than a shade of arrogance on their behalf. Big Jack wasn't a great talker and preferred to call a 'spade a shovel'. He could be blunt and had difficulty accepting the perceived bias of London based journalists. He openly resented the money 'southern boxers' like Walker earned, feeling he deserved just as much, and believed he never seemed to get any acknowledgment for his good performances.

As an amateur light heavyweight he'd won the ABA title and earned himself a bronze medal at the European championships. Even though he'd been a professional less than half the time of Henry, he'd actually engaged in one more fight, forty nine in total. He'd suffered less defeats as well – eight, but rather surprisingly there had been only two mutual opponents. Bodell had been outpointed by Joe Erskine and knocked out in six rounds by Hubert Hilton. Ominously for Bodell, of his losses, the one to Erskine was the only time he wasn't knocked out! He was big and strong, an awkward southpaw, and brave. He'd won his last twelve fights, and although not a devastating puncher, he'd stopped more than his fair share with an accumulation of solid blows from his southpaw stance. He would pose a significant threat if Cooper had indeed lost his edge.

Cooper, who'd set up camp in Chislehurst, had been sparring with young heavyweight Roy Enifer, a good solid southpaw who could emulate Bodell's style. Cooper would weigh five pounds lighter than he'd been only eight weeks before, for the Jacobs fight, and this helped dispel any thoughts he was finished.

Bodell came out at the first bell cheered on by a majority of the 10,000 crowd, and launched into attack throwing long left handers, forcing Henry to defend. Cooper would later claim he was simply trying to gauge the challenger's weaknesses. It obviously didn't take him long to work things out! Midway through the second round Cooper caught Bodell flush on the chin with a short left hook, the effect of which wasn't immediately noticeable. The challenger stopped charging forward, obviously a bit more wary of what the champion could do. Shortly after, a similar punch landed, and now the fans realised that Bodell was looking a bit unsteady on his feet. Henry knew Bodell was in trouble and went for the finish. Another full blooded left hook had the Derbyshire man staggering into the ropes and then stumbling backwards like a drunk trying to avoid the inevitable. When Bodell found himself trapped in the corner, a long right hand punch from Cooper landed on the unprotected jaw and just before the referee dived in to stop it, another left hook landed, to add the finishing touch. The second notch was on a third Lonsdale belt, and Henry had proved beyond doubt that as far as domestic opposition was concerned, he was still top of the tree.

Plans were already in motion for Cooper's next outing. There was an offer of £18,000 from Germany for a challenge to Mildenberger, and Alex Griffiths, reviewing the success of the promotion at Wolverhampton, was also considering making an offer. Meanwhile Levene, benefitting from the success of the Walker v Mildenberger contest at Wembley, entered the fray. Typically for Wicks, knowing he was once again in the driving seat, announced to the press he'd accept nothing less than £20,000 for Henry's next fight.

The world heavyweight title was now in a state of utter chaos. Ali, on refusing to step forward and be inducted into the US army, was 'stripped' of his championship. The WBA were putting together a tournament featuring the leading contenders to decide who'd take his place. Among those believed to be involved in this was Karl Mildenberger. The EBU instructed Mildenberger to defend against Gerhard Zech and when he refused, they declared the title vacant, and proposed that Cooper and Zech should be matched to decide their new champion. Wicks wasn't interested. A huge 'money' fight was in the offing against the 'Golden Boy' Billy Walker, subject to Board approval.

In August the Board sanctioned the Cooper v Walker match, and the 'big' fight was on. It was set for 7 November at Wembley, and to prove Walker's popularity each fighter would receive £25,000, contrary to the usual arrangement when the champion would receive a 60% share of the purse.

In September, as expected, Mildenberger was included in the WBA tournament, losing to Bonavena at the first hurdle, and inexplicably, the EBU returned his European title, because he now agreed to defend against Zech.

It's difficult to imagine just how big a star Billy Walker was in the 1960s. In many ways he was a product of his time. For the first fifteen or so years after the Second World War, Britain was a relatively austere place. The country was in debt to America for 'war loans'. Houses and factories had been flattened by German bombs, and food rationing existed until 1948.

By 1960 a new generation of young people, who'd never experienced war at first hand, were beginning to see a new way of life emerging. These were exciting times. New musical sounds were heard; clothes were no longer simple necessities of life, but items of fashion; hair styles were deemed to be outrageous; motor cars were becoming affordable for ordinary people; many homes had replaced their old radio sets with television; people began to have telephones installed in their house, and as Prime Minister Harold MacMillan stated – "We've never had it so good".

Into this changing world appeared Billy Walker. The handsome 'Blonde Bomber' with the knockout punch, who'd famously flattened a huge American in front of the TV cameras, in an amateur international which saw a 10-0 whitewash for the British team, was a promoter's dream. He was persuaded to turn professional almost immediately by Harry Levene and Jarvis Astaire, being tied to a huge £9,000 contract (worth £185,000 in 2016). Walker continued to excite the public but his performances didn't exactly match the money he was earning. The 'Golden Boy' didn't get the time to learn his trade, as other new professionals would have. Every fight was a major event. His opponents weren't selected with a view to help him learn new skills, simply to provide an exciting event for the paying public. With the result, by the time he faced Henry, from twenty eight fights he'd lost eight and drawn two. Only in his last contest with Mildenberger was a title on the line. He'd lost to Johnny Prescott in a re-match and also to Brian London. In fact after the Cooper fight he'd have only two more bouts, and then he was out of the game for good. But what an exciting fighter he was. The fans knew he'd quite happily take two punches to land one, and was value for money.

Cooper approached the fight using his tried and tested routine. He was once again based at the Bull's Head hotel in Chislehurst, running in the early hours while trainer Danny Holland cycled alongside, then on to the Thomas a' Becket where he'd train and spar. Jim Wicks imported tough Spaniard, Mariano Echevarria, and invited Rocky Campbell and Rocky James down from the Midlands as sparring partners. He was also considering using amateur heavyweight, Billy Wells, the intention being that each would spar one round at a time against Cooper, on a daily basis. Walker meantime was similarly engaged in early morning runs with trainer Freddie Hill and sparring at the new Board of Control gym on Haverstock Hill.

Interest in the fight was huge with the venue being quickly sold out. The week before the contest the BBC approached Levene and offered him £21,000(£350,000 in 2016) for permission to show the fight live. All parties to the promotion agreed but the Board of Control rejected the proposal claiming it would set a precedent that might ultimately affect attendances at future promotions. The BBC offer, to show highlights the following evening, was reduced to £11,000.

This fight was an opportunity for Cooper to secure an unprecedented third Lonsdale belt. A win would also complete a set of victories over the second generation of British heavyweights who believed they could put an end to the Cooper reign. Henry had disposed of the first generation in the shapes of Erskine, London and Richardson. During the second phase he'd already stopped both Prescott and Bodell, with only Walker now remaining.

On the night Cooper was the overwhelming favourite, but Walker had a large and vociferous following many of whom held a sincere belief this could be the night the 'Blonde Bomber' finally came good. During the first couple of rounds it looked as if Walker had been instructed to abandon his usual battle plan of all out attack and try to box his way into range. At the same time Cooper seemed to have adopted a more cautious approach, firing out jabs to find his distance but without risking throwing the left hook. The fans should have known Walker couldn't maintain this way of fighting. In the third round the 'Golden Boy' opened up, going all out for the quick win, and had some success in the process. Cooper was troubled with one particular assault while on the ropes, and had to fight his way out. The crowd were on their feet and the challenger probably took the round.

In the fifth round, with Cooper now back in control, boxing steadily behind the jab and landing the occasional vicious left hook, a cut suddenly appeared over Walker's right eye. In the corner before the next round Jim Wicks simply reminded Henry that he should know what to do now given that he'd been on the receiving end on numerous occasions. For as long as the sixth round lasted Cooper jabbed and jabbed at Walker's bleeding eyebrow, some estimates suggest that in less than two minutes he landed around thirty unanswered punches. The referee took one quick look, and stopped the carnage. A third belt was strapped around Cooper's waist.

There is an interesting historical footnote with regard to Cooper's Lonsdale belts. The first one he secured outright in 1961 had been originally commissioned before the war and was made of pure gold. After 1945 gold became too expensive, and from that year the Lonsdale belt comprised of silver gilt.

Being interviewed immediately after the fight, Cooper gave a clear indication of which direction his boxing career would take. He stated that the public were unlikely to see him back in the ring defending his British title but he'd pursue a match with Karl Mildenberger for the European crown, one that had been taken from him, unfairly, as far as he was concerned. There were also new press reports suggesting that regardless of the outcome against Mildenberger, he'd retire during 1968.

Just round the corner there would be a huge endorsement of just how popular Henry was in the eyes of the British public in general. In the 1960s the BBC Sports Personality of the Year programme was watched by over 20 million viewers. In those days all sports were covered by the BBC, and each November a panel of experts would select ten sports stars and ask the public to vote on who they thought was their sports personality of the year. The results were kept a closely guarded secret until the night of the programme and every national newspaper would speculate on who would win. The winner in the previous year was Bobby Moore, being the captain of the England side which had won the World Cup. No boxer had ever won it.

When Henry arrived that night at the BBC Theatre in London, he was advised he was in the top three, and should start preparing a short speech. Show jumper Harvey Smith was named in third place, cyclist Beryl Burton came in second, and much to the joy of the boxing public, Henry came away with the iconic trophy. A fitting end to an extremely successful year.

Action from the 1956 fight with Peter Bates. (Courtesy of Boxing News)

Richardson's knocked out and 'Henry's hammer' is born. (Courtesy of Boxing News)

Joe Erskine shows his skill and avoids the left hook. (Courtesy of Boxing News)

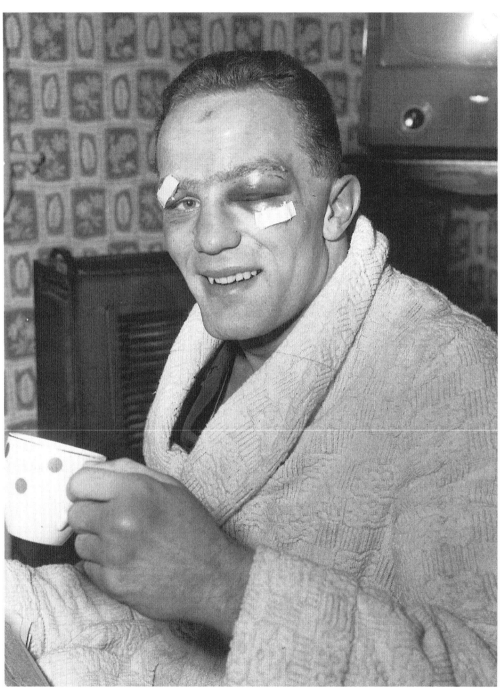

What it looks like to be a winner! Henry, the morning after winning the British title against Brian London in 1959. (Courtesy of Boxing News)

Gawie de Klerk has just felt the power of 'Henry's hammer'. (Courtesy of Boxing News)

Cooper running, with Danny Holland on the bike. (Courtesy of Derek Rowe)

The 'horrible' knockout of Joe Erskine in 1959. (Courtesy of Boxing News)

Henry with his first Lonsdale belt 1961. (Courtesy of Boxing News)

Cooper on his back at the end of the disastrous loss to Zora Folley 1961. (Courtesy of Boxing News)

Cooper's perfect left jab against the unfortunate Richardson 1963. (Courtesy of Boxing News)

Cooper and Ali after their world title fight 1966. (Courtesy of Derek Rowe)

The 'famous' three Lonsdale belts photo 1967. (Courtesy of Derek Rowe)

Mildenberger goes down on one knee 1968. (Courtesy of Boxing News)

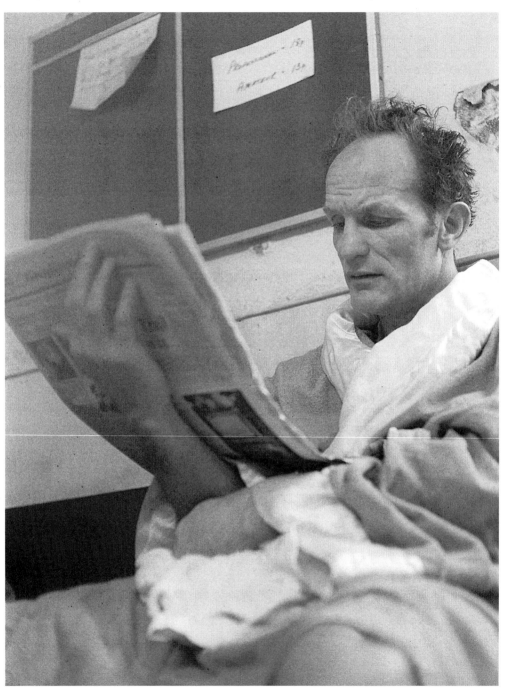

Cooper after training prior to Bodell fight, 1970. (Courtesy of Derek Rowe)

Urtain covers up from a Cooper barrage, 1970. (Private Collection)

The last image of Cooper in a boxing ring, following defeat by Bugner, 1971. (Courtesy of Boxing News)

CHAPTER 13

The Fight that Never Happened

ALTHOUGH COOPER MADE IT CLEAR HE'D BE SEEKING A FIGHT WITH KARL Mildenberger for the European title, and the money involved was likely to be highly rewarding, it must have seemed pretty obvious his career was approaching the final phase. Three Lonsdale belts were secured, there were no obvious challengers in Britain (he'd beaten them all!), he was a relatively rich man, and due to his growing public popularity, the outlook for promotional work was very favourable. His ageing body, after seventeen years as an amateur and professional, was showing signs of stress. Now in addition to his damaged elbow and fist, Cooper was suffering from a knee injury, suspected to be cartilage trouble, necessitating cortisone injections to control the pain. Little did anyone realise however, not even Cooper himself, or Jim Wicks, that retirement was still an incredible three years away.

Behind the scenes Cooper was having a difficult time. As well as having treatment on his knee he was losing out on advertising opportunities because he had to spend so much time working in the greengrocers business, as it was starting to go under. While Henry had his own problems, the British heavyweight scene was also in a state of turmoil. Rival promoters were endeavouring to stage their own elimination contests with a view to creating a legitimate challenger for Cooper's title. On one side of the equation were Bodell, London, Carl Gizzi and Billy Gray while George Walker was demanding the Board should force a re-match between his brother and Henry. The world title scene was in similar disarray. Ali's former sparring partner and friend, Jimmy Ellis, had just outpointed Jerry Quarry to claim the WBA version of the title, while Joe Frazier knocked out Buster Mathis to win the title recognised by the New York State Athletic Commission. What a mess!

As early as April, given that the proposed fight was still five months away, it was announced publicly that Henry would indeed fight Mildenberger although no venue had been decided. Apparently a fight before then could not be arranged because of

Cooper's tax concerns. The British heavyweight scene continued to change as managers and promoters vied to get their favourite into the leading position to challenge Cooper. Most of the motivation for those involved was the belief that Henry would retire after the Mildenberger fight and they were desperate to get their boxer recommended to fight for the vacant belt. Part of this plan saw Jack Bodell stop Brian London, and now the Board instructed him to fight Carl Gizzi in a final eliminator.

By the middle of August contracts had been signed for the European title fight to be held at Wembley on 18 September, with Cooper attracting a purse of £20,000. That figure was significant, because in the same week the details of the fight were formally announced, Angelo Dundee contacted Jim Wicks with a view to a WBA title fight between his boxer, Jimmy Ellis, and Cooper. Quick as a flash Wicks responded with a demand for £40,000 for his man, before he'd even consider the offer further!

Cooper continued with his normal routine in preparation for the championship contest, basing himself in Chislehurst, while as the date of the fight approached, Mildenberger arrived in London and began training at the same gym as Walker had done, in Haverstock Hill. Wicks advertised for southpaw sparring partners and Londoner Des Cox was one of those who answered the call.

Mildenberger had a long and distinguished career. From sixty one fights he'd won fifty three, lost five, and the remainder were drawn. He'd been European champion for four years and taken Ali to the twelfth round before being stopped in his only world title challenge. He'd notable wins over Wayne Bethea, Pete Rademacher and Eddie Machen, as well as a draw with Zora Folley. Seven British boxers had fought Mildenberger and he'd lost only to Dick Richardson via first round knockout in 1962. The German was a good boxer but with only nineteen wins inside the distance, he didn't seem to possess a knockout punch. He certainly wasn't coming to London to lose, with two busloads of supporters intent on travelling all the way from Frankfurt.

Mildenberger entered the ring more than a stone and a half heavier than Cooper but it didn't prove advantageous. This proved to be an outstanding performance by the British champion, possibly the best of his career. Right from the first bell Henry took the initiative jabbing and moving, keeping the experienced German off balance.

Henry Cooper: Cut Eyes and Left Hooks

Cooper had mastered the one technique necessary to nullify a southpaw, continual movement to his left away from the big left hand punches. The second round, unfortunately, saw the 'other' side of Henry in similar circumstances to previous misdemeanours against Erskine and London. The rather inept Italian referee moved in to break the boxers up and as he stepped back to allow them to continue Cooper landed with a huge left hook on the exposed jaw of Mildenberger. This was against the rules, and as the referee began to warn Cooper, the stunned German flopped down on one knee. Astonishingly the referee looked round and began to count over Mildenberger. The champion got to his feet at the count of eight.

Cooper continued to score freely and controlled the action, with Mildenberger perhaps winning the fourth round due to his aggression. The German looked to be slightly shorter than Cooper and when he moved forward he did so with his head down leading to several warnings from the referee. In the sixth round, the referee stepped in quickly, as Mildenberger could clearly be seen rubbing the inside of his glove up over Cooper's vulnerable eyebrows. On another occasion while in a clinch the German moved his forehead across Cooper's face with the apparent intention of causing damage. All of this did nothing to upset Henry's rhythm as he continued to move freely firing off jabs to the head and body with the occasional right cross thrown in. In the seventh round a 'legal' left hook landed, and this time Mildenberger was legitimately felled. He rose at the count of two but the large 10,000 crowd anticipated the end was fast approaching. The eighth round turned out to be the last as Henry got up onto his toes and danced around the forlorn, soon to be ex-champion, landing freely with quick, but light jabs. Seconds before the bell sounded, heads clashed again, and Cooper was cut above the eye. Henry went back to his corner, the referee examined the damage, and amid confusion, raised Cooper's hand in victory.

BBC commentator Harry Carpenter told the viewers that the referee had invoked an EBU rule whereby if a title fight goes over the halfway stage and a fighter is retired due to an accidental head clash, the fighter leading on points gets the verdict. In fact that was not the case. It was announced officially as a disqualification win. Either way, Henry was now a triple champion, winning in fine style. There could be no better accolade than Mildenberger claiming years later that Henry was the best boxer he'd ever faced, with the exception of Ali. High praise indeed.

There could surely now have been no question of Cooper considering retirement. Such was his popularity and the demand to see him in action that it wouldn't have made sense to even consider that course of action. When the figures were collated, 14 million viewers tuned into the BBC Sportsview programme to see the Mildenberger fight.

Towards the end of November Jim Wicks announced there would be a European title defence against Piero Tomasoni in Italy sometime in February of the following year, and the Boxing News got involved by organising a package holiday to Rome for the 'Cooper fan club'. The victory over Mildenberger lifted Cooper, at the ripe old age of thirty four, back into the world top ten rankings, and with Jack Bodell winning a final eliminator over Carl Gizzi, he'd soon be required to meet that demand also.

Official acknowledgement of just how popular Henry was in the eyes of the British public was just around the corner. In the Queen's New Year's honours list was the name of Henry Cooper, awarded the OBE for services to boxing.

Several days later the Boxing News announced they had found enough fans to fill two aircraft for the trip to Rome for Cooper's European defence on 27 February. British boxers, Vic Andreeti, Carl Gizzi and Walter McGowan were added to the bill, and the BBC was going to cover the show live for their viewers.

Things didn't go to plan however. Soon after the Cooper team set up camp at the Bull's Head, Henry injured his big toe, which soon became infected. Just a fortnight before the contest, journalists who had attended the hotel for a brewery event, noticed Cooper was limping, and it came as no surprise to learn that a doctor had ordered a postponement. The fight was re-arranged for 13 March. At the time Jim Wicks told reporters that as Henry couldn't train properly his weight was rising and he wouldn't risk the European title unless he was fully fit. But was it just a coincidence that Cooper and is family were in the midst of being fitted out, and making preparations, for the forthcoming investiture at Buckingham Palace on 17 February?

Tomasoni was a relatively light punching heavyweight with most of his stoppage wins coming early in his career when the opposition was weaker. He'd earned the right to challenge Cooper by beating Jurgen Blin on a disqualification. He'd twice lost on points to Mildenberger, but had knocked out Jack Bodell and beaten Hubert Hilton on points. He wasn't an awe inspiring threat to Henry, in fact the biggest

Henry Cooper: Cut Eyes and Left Hooks

danger was that the fight was in Italy, and most pundits reckoned he'd have to knock the Italian out to retain his title. They weren't far off the mark as it transpired!

As a further measure of Cooper's growing popularity at this late stage of his career, the Boxing News which had arrived on the newsstands every Friday for over sixty years, was published a day later than usual, to allow an up to date report of the fight to be included.

What happened in that Roman ring in front of 15,000 Italians and a few hundred Brits, could not have been referred to as either a bout or a contest, it was pure and simply a fight! Clearly Tomasoni realised he had no chance of out boxing Cooper, his only option was to take the fight into the 'trenches'. Every one of the five rounds the fight lasted was packed with incident.

Tomasoni emerged from his corner at the sound of the first bell with his head down and arms flailing, forcing Cooper onto the ropes. The champion pushed Tomasoni back into the centre of the ring where a left hook to the body and one to head sent the Italian crashing to the canvas. In round two Tomasoni threw a suspiciously low left hook into Cooper's midriff and Henry sunk to the floor holding his groin. The Cooper corner and ringsiders from Britain jumped to their feet in protest and almost collapsed in astonishment when Ben Brill the Dutch referee began to count. Henry struggled to his feet in obvious pain, but his temper soon took over as he stormed after Tomasoni landing cleanly with a left hook and right cross hurting the challenger.

Incredibly, the third round mirrored what had happened previously. Cooper had been advised by his corner to jab and jab in an effort to keep the Italian off, but Tomasoni hadn't read the script. He again tore into Cooper winging wild punches from all directions and yet another low blow landed, doubling Henry up and forcing him to crouch on the canvas. As Cooper held his injured groin Mr Brill started counting again, considering the punch a legitimate blow. When the fight continued Tomasoni charged again, and this time received what appeared to be a public warning from the referee who was fast losing control. Despite the warning, more of the same ensued in the next round, resulting in both boxers tumbling to the floor in a heap. Cooper and Tomasoni were warned by the referee, and shortly after, the challenger was once again cautioned for a low blow.

The excited Italian crowd, fearing their man would be disqualified, started a fearful demonstration with those at ringside being pelted with anything the fans could get their hands on, forcing a thirty second delay in the fight before order could be restored. In the corner between rounds the Cooper team must have feared the worse. The potential outcome was there for all to see. With an intimidated referee there was no way he'd disqualify Tomasoni. If by any stretch of the imagination the fight went the full fifteen rounds who on earth could believe, with the hostile crowd, that Cooper would get the decision. It was more likely the referee would disqualify Henry at the first opportunity. There could only be one answer favourable to Cooper, and he delivered it in the next round!

Henry came straight out the corner and threw a fast left hook to the head and Tomasoni dropped like a stone clutching Cooper around the legs. The Italian was on his knees and fell back supported by a hand resting on the canvas. He hadn't moved from that position when the relieved Mr Brill counted him out. The crowd, who, remember, knew Henry's wife was Italian, amazingly gave the British fighter a standing ovation which simply underlined what a bizarre night it had been for all concerned. Two weeks later the BBC announced that the fight attracted 18.5 million viewers, the largest for any programme that week.

In the week that followed, the Italian promoter who put on the 'contest', indicated he was attempting to have the WBA champ, Jimmy Ellis, defend his crown against Cooper in Rome. No one then could've predicted the future significance to Cooper of the suggestion. Just a few days prior to this the British Boxing Board had issued a press release stating that, along with the fledgling World Boxing Council and five American states including New York, they'd reached a decision, following a reluctant acceptance that Ali had actually 'retired'. They declared that Joe Frazier should meet the number one contender so that there would be clarity as to who held the world title. If that contender should not be the WBA champion, Jimmy Ellis, then the winner of that particular contest must meet Ellis in their first defence.

In the middle of April storm clouds were forming around Cooper's future. In a less than subtle move to put pressure on the British Boxing Board of Control, promoter Jack Solomons held a press conference at the Strand Palace Hotel attended by Cooper and Wicks. He told the assembled audience he'd arranged for Jimmy Ellis to defend his WBA title against Henry in either June or September and indicated he'd been in talks with promoters in Sweden, Italy, France and Ireland regarding potential venues for the contest. He would also consider the 18,000 seat Earls Court Exhibition Hall, but indicated the major snag with this plan was the Board's insistence that they wouldn't recognise the match up as being for the world title.

The cunning old promoter also linked up a telephone line to Miami which was amplified so the press could hear the conversation he was having with Ellis's manager, Angelo Dundee. Dundee said that Ellis was prepared to fight anywhere in Europe. Thereafter the leading boxing correspondents were invited to speak to Dundee to allow them to produce further newspaper columns, hopefully as far as Solomons was concerned, in support of his project. Was it a coincidence that on the very day of the press conference, the Boxing Board produced a bulletin instructing Cooper to defend his British title against Jack Bodell, who to be fair, had earned the right, with recent wins over Gizzi and Walker.

Solomons increased the pressure on the Board by announcing the fight would take place on 21 June and asked them to accept it as being for the world championship. In response, the Board made it clear they were affiliated to the WBC and that this organisation had made their decision. They went further and pointed out that the WBC was a truly world organisation with affiliates from the Far East and South America, as well as support from the European Boxing Union and the British Empire Committee. The WBA in contrast, they said, was an organisation supported by a few minor states in America (in fact there were forty five states supporting them!). They did offer to canvas the WBC to gain support for a Cooper v Ellis fight as being a final eliminating contest, with the winner mandated to fight Frazier.

The boxing journalists in the national press, seemingly supported by the British public, were outraged, calling the Board's decision a disgrace. At the time Britain had no world champions at any weight and they argued this was a clear opportunity for the 'nation's favourite sports personality' to alter that situation. They further pointed out that Cooper's fights had generated huge sums in commissions for the Board, and he'd been an outstanding ambassador for professional boxing in the country for nigh on fifteen years. Henry himself made it clear that win, lose or draw, he'd retire after the bout, causing the public to feel further aggrieved that the Board should deprive him of the opportunity of finally winning the world title.

In a final effort to force the Board to change their mind, several hundred supporters and numerous cameramen lined the streets around the Boxing Board offices as Cooper and Wicks arrived to formally present a letter informing them that he'd given up his British title. It takes people of strong character, in the face of so much pressure, to stick to a decision which would adversely affect the most popular sports personality in the country, and to alienate some of the most influential members of their organisation – but stick to it, they did! In theory, you can't lose something you don't have, but Solomons, Wicks, Cooper, Ellis, Dundee and a host of others, including, perversely, the Board themselves, lost the opportunity to earn huge sums of money on what was basically a 'point of principal'.

Into this impasse stepped rival promoter Harry Levene who, refusing to be intimidated by officialdom, announced that the Cooper v Ellis battle would take place on 27 September at Wembley with live TV showing the fight in colour for the first time. There were now insinuations that Wicks wouldn't pay the Board's commission for the fight and when pressed on this he told listening journalists that this would have to be met by Levene. In mid August, in front of the BBC cameras, both Ellis (pictures beamed from Miami) and Cooper signed the contracts for their forthcoming fight.

Sadly, trouble was brewing within the very tight Cooper circle. Danny Holland had been with the team as trainer and cut man for fifteen years. Trainers usually accepted 10% of the boxer's purse, but in later years Henry would state that as his purses grew Holland received a lesser percentage. The reason for this was the considerable amount of expenses for his training camps, and the fact that the massive size of Henry's purses made it unrealistic for the trainer to expect to receive the normal 10% payment. It appears Holland had been unhappy with this deal for years and it'd been a continual source of disagreement between him and Wicks, with Henry taking a back seat. The end came when plans were being made for the Ellis fight. Henry's purse was to be in the region of £20,000 but Holland was being offered £600. This was the 'straw that broke the camel's back', and Holland walked away.

With the fight only three weeks away, and the camp already set up as usual in Chislehurst, Henry was doing his 'party piece' of Cossack dancing for some journalists when his knee gave way. A visit to a specialist revealed a cartilage was damaged. Initially the world title fight was postponed for a couple of weeks but when a further examination revealed that surgery was the only option, the contest had to be cancelled. The recovery period wasn't as straight forward as Cooper thought, and it took several weeks of intensive rehabilitation at the home of Arsenal football club before he was back to fitness. By this point Wicks knew that there was no chance of Cooper fighting again until 1970, and along with the loss of the Ellis fight, the European crown had also to be surrendered.

Wicks still held out some hope that the world title fight could be rearranged, perhaps in the summer, but discussions had already begun for Ellis to finally meet Joe Frazier, a fight which would resolve the dispute over who would take over Ali's mantle once and for all.

1969 came to an end, indeed the 1960s came to an end, with a new British heavyweight champion on the throne – Jack Bodell. The big man from Swadlincote won the vacant title in October by beating Carl Gizzi, and Levene was already in negotiations for him to challenge for the European title. At this point nobody really knew where Henry's Empire title lay!!!

CHAPTER 14

Unforgettable Ending

PEOPLE CAN'T PREDICT THE FUTURE WITH CERTAINTY BUT IN JANUARY 1970 Ron Olver at the Boxing News seemed to have gained access to a crystal ball! Included in his section was an interview with Cooper. Henry was asked what he thought of the young heavyweight, Joe Bugner. Cooper said, "I rate him still as a very good prospect. You've got to realise he's still a kid – still a boy. He's only nineteen. He's got another two, three, four or five years in front of him just learning his business. He'll be OK if he is taught to relax. At the moment I think he's still a little bit too tense. I think they've told him to keep his elbows in to stop those punches to the body and I think he's holding himself too rigid. If he can learn to relax in the ring I think he'll take his opportunities quicker because he's more relaxed. He's that tense that he's missing chances and opportunities." Given what was to happen in just over twelve months, perhaps Henry should have kept his views to himself!

Harry Levene and Jim Wicks were already in discussions concerning Cooper's next fight, and after his cartilage operation, it could reasonably have been considered more of a comeback. Levene had pre-booked the Empire Pool at Wembley for 24 March and intended promoting a contest between Henry and the new British champion, Jack Bodell. Wicks was soon to discover what it's like to sit on the wrong side of the negotiating table. He demanded the heavy end of the purse for Cooper and wanted the fight to be over twelve rounds. George Biddles, Bodell's manager, was having none of it. He claimed Bodell had been 'messed around' for years having to beat London, Walker and Gizzi to get a title shot, and as champion he was entitled to a 60%-40% split of the purse. When discussions broke down, the Board intervened and announced they were not prepared to force Bodell to fight anyone in particular, as long as they approved of any subsequent challenger. Biddles then advised the press that Bodell would travel to America in February to fight Jerry Quarry.

Henry Cooper: Cut Eyes and Left Hooks

Somebody obviously backed down because Levene quickly confirmed that Cooper would indeed fight Bodell on the original date, with both boxers sharing £30,000. There was no mention of how this figure would be split, but it's likely a compromise was reached whereby the purse was divided equally. Levene also announced that the contest would be over fifteen rounds for the British and Empire titles. This seemed to clarify that Cooper was still Empire champion, although no one seemed to have been sure.

On the day contracts were signed for the contest, proved an example of how the modern world of communications would likely have ruined 'the surprise'. A small press conference had been arranged featuring Cooper, Bodell and Levene, with Wicks and Biddles in the background. Unknown to all those involved except Henry, was the fact that later in the evening Eamon Andrews would appear from nowhere with his famous 'red book' and invite Cooper to join him and the guests at Thames TV studios for an edition of the extremely popular programme, "This is your Life". It must have been extremely uncomfortable for Bodell who'd to give the impression at the press conference that he was angry at the way the negotiations for the fight had progressed, while at the same time, he'd secretly been invited to be, basically, a 'cheerleader' that evening to celebrate Cooper's life.

The beginning of the year also heralded the partial end of another generation of British heavyweights with the defeat of Johnny Prescott by Bugner. 'Partial' only because the single thread leading back all those years to 1954 still existed, in the shape of Brian London. The first generation including Erskine and Richardson were long gone and now the second generation of Walker and Prescott had also retired. London and Bodell provided the link to the third generation of heavyweight challengers to emerge during Cooper's career, consisting primarily of Bugner and Danny McAlinden.

Young sports fans today would not recognise the sporting culture which existed in 1970. During pre-fight preliminaries at a boxing show in the Royal Albert Hall the now retired Billy Walker received a tremendous ovation as he was introduced to the crowd. When Jack Bodell was similarly invited up into the ring he was loudly booed. This caused an outcry among the press and ringside officials. Colin Hart, writing in the SUN wrote that he felt ashamed to be a Londoner, while the editor of the Boxing News added, "These so-called sportsmen who booed Bodell should be ashamed of themselves. Jack Bodell is a credit to boxing. A fine sportsman, who always gives of his best".

Coming into the Bodell fight, Cooper must have been in a very contented frame of mind. He'd shown, since the devastating loss to Patterson almost three and a half years previously that he could still cope with the top heavyweights in Britain and Europe. Outside the ring his celebrity status was ensuring he could begin to visualise a financially lucrative career once he hung up the gloves. Henry was taking part in numerous ventures on radio and television. He was a 'team captain' on the extremely popular 'Question of Sport' BBC programme, and appeared regularly in TV commercials. Up until then, without these opportunities, there must have been background pressure in relation to what the future would hold should a defeat bring a premature end to his boxing career. No such worry now existed.

As the Cooper team, now minus Danny Holland, once again based themselves in Chislehurst they would have known that this would be a different Bodell to the one they faced at Wolverhampton in June 1967. This time the Derbyshire man was the champion and that status would bring extra confidence and determination to his performance. At the Thomas a' Becket Henry was using as sparring partners, Des Cox (whose own career had seemingly ended in September 1968), Roger Tighe, a useful southpaw from Hull, and Richard Dunn, another southpaw, who would go on to be British, European and Commonwealth (Empire) champion, before famously fighting Ali for the world title. This was ideal preparation.

Bodell, too, brought in quality sparring in the shape of rising stars, Danny McAlinden and Bunny Johnson. Bizarrely, McAlinden would knock out Bodell to win the British and Commonwealth titles, Johnson would do the same to McAlinden, and Dunn, in turn, would beat Johnson, for the same titles, all within the next five years!!

Since losing to Cooper, Bodell had gone on a tremendous run of form. He'd won all twelve fights, seven inside the distance. Not only had he won the British title but he'd out fought, and stopped, Billy Walker in a hugely exciting contest, also beating rated American Jose Roman, a future world title challenger. Bodell was ready for this fight!

Despite being only a few weeks short of his thirty sixth birthday, and having not fought fifteen rounds for six years, the press were unanimous that Cooper would win. They did suggest however that if Henry didn't finish it early, he could struggle in the latter stages. With Danny Holland missing, Eddie Thomas was drafted in to look after the Cooper eyebrows.

The bout turned out to be a tough and gruelling affair for both men. Although Henry won comfortably there was little doubt age was catching up fast. He was a fraction slower with his punches, he looked heavier on his feet, and in the late rounds he could be seen on occasion gasping for breath. When the bell sounded to end the fight Cooper's eyes were sunk in his head and he looked gaunt. Nevertheless, he'd performed admirably. Henry controlled the fight from beginning to end and from the scorecards it seemed that Bodell may only have won three rounds. Cooper had 'big' rounds in the seventh and twelfth. In the former, a short left hook, very similar to the one which caused all the damage in their first fight, brought Bodell to a sudden stop before he slumped to the canvas on his knees. The referee didn't count and when Bodell rose, he simply motioned for the fight to continue. Shortly after, following another 'tasty' left hander, Cooper threw Bodell to the floor and this time the referee DID count, though why, is inexplicable. In the twelfth round, Cooper again landed with that vicious short left hook and the tiring Bodell stumbled to the floor. A short count was administered. Midway through the last round the Wembley crowd were on their feet knowing that their hero had regained the British title, a feat not repeated since 1938.

Amazingly, after sixteen years as a professional, Cooper was ranked as the number eight contender for Joe Frazier's world crown (he'd knocked out Ellis in a unification fight). As the Cooper family flew off for a well deserved holiday in Portugal events were unfolding which would have an effect on the remainder of his career.

In April, Jose Manuel Urtain, knocked out Peter Weiland in Madrid to win the vacant European title, and retained it two months later in Barcelona against another German, Jurgen Blin. Back home, the young Adonis, Joe Bugner, stopped veteran Brian London in the fifth round. The EBU now nominated Cooper as the mandatory contender for Urtain's crown, and Bugner was being viewed as the heir to Henry's British throne. The Bugner fight with London was also quite significant for Henry in a nostalgic way. After the contest Brian London took the microphone and told the crowd it was his final fight. London was the last, excluding Henry himself, of the 'gang of four' who'd set out in the mid 1950s with such high hopes. London and

Erskine had been British champions and Richardson won the European title. London fought boxers from the 'three generations' of British heavyweights – Erskine, Richardson, Prescott, Walker, Bodell and finally Bugner. Henry would join him in that group in less than a year.

Harry Levene had an horrendous battle to get the Spaniard Urtain's name onto a contract for his defence against Cooper. The veteran promoter travelled to Spain in an effort to clinch the deal but it seemed Urtain was avoiding him. Levene travelled to a meeting in Madrid only to be advised he had now to go to Barcelona. Eventually he gave up and returned home.

Levene was incensed, but not beaten. He approached Wicks and tried to get him to agree to Henry fighting the German Jurgen Blin on the scheduled date. Levene intended making a request to the EBU to have Urtain stripped of his title and having the proposed match with Blin being sanctioned for the vacant crown. Jim Wicks refused.

The EBU put the fight out to purse bids and Levene took the unusual step of bypassing the British Boxing Board and instead travelled to Rome, hand delivering his bid, apparently to a round of applause from the EBU officials! The bid for the contract was £68,000(just over £1 million in 2016), the biggest offer Levene had ever placed on a fight up till then.

Levene's difficulties didn't end there. He still had to get Urtain's signature on a contract, so he travelled out to Paris with British Boxing Board secretary, Teddy Waltham. They met Urtain and his manager, who both were obviously overjoyed at his side of the deal which amounted to £40,800 (£600,000). He still wouldn't sign the contract until his lawyer had seen it, possibly because he couldn't believe his luck! A short time later, when Levene threatened to cancel the whole affair, he eventually put pen to paper. Incredibly matters were still not finalised. Urtain wanted to arrive in London the day before the fight. Waltham advised him that the Board usually required foreign boxers to arrive in the country ten days prior to a contest. Finally, with patience running out, an compromise was reached whereby Urtain would fly in six days beforehand.

Urtain had built a huge reputation for himself. In just less than two and a half years, he'd taken part in an astonishing thirty five fights. In contrast, over the same period, Cooper had fought three times! The man from the Basque country had thirty

Henry Cooper: Cut Eyes and Left Hooks

four wins, the vast majority by knockout. His sole defeat was by disqualification. Of course bland statistics don't tell the full story. No one with even a superficial knowledge of heavyweight boxing would have recognised any of his opponents other than Jose Peyre, until he won the European title from Weiland. Obviously Blin, whom he defended against, was a 'known' fighter, and he beat him on points. The great interest in Urtain came from his physical strength and relative punching power, gained apparently from his days engaged in the Basque sport of stone lifting. He was a good four inches shorter than Cooper but built like an ox.

For the first time in British boxing history the result of the bout would be decided not simply by the referee , but a further two judges sitting at ringside, a recent rule brought in by the EBU. The packed Wembley crowd were hoping the judges wouldn't be needed. The first round suggested the champion was a bit crude but a reasonably competent fighter. He winged big right hand swings, one of which opened a cut over Henry's left eye bringing a sense of foreboding to his supporters. Cooper always preferred taller boxers, and although his jabs were finding the target, the left hooks would go sailing over Urtain's head. Cooper took the round, but it was close, and the Spaniard looked dangerous.

Eddie Thomas dealt efficiently with the cut and during the second round Cooper was much quicker, with the left jab beginning to have an impact. By the third round Henry was in command and the champion looked totally incapable of avoiding the jab, with Cooper beginning to throw big left hooks, most just narrowly missing the target. With the fourth round under way it was clear that Urtain was out of his depth as he had no answer to Cooper's skilful boxing. Matters got worse for the Spaniard in the fifth round when a left hook cum uppercut smashed into his nose, possibly even breaking it, as the blood started to flow. Even though Cooper was cut over the right eye in the sixth round he was in no danger, and vicious hooks into Urtain's midriff were taking the wind out of him. The eighth round was scrappy but in the last minute the referee issued a public warning to Urtain for illegal use of the head, and with his right eye visibly closing due to a swelling he looked a sorrowful figure when the bell sounded.

Confusion reigned in the Spaniard's corner as they seemed to be trying to attract the referee's attention probably to withdraw their man. However the bell rang and Urtain was back on his feet prepared to fight on, but within seconds the referee waved it over and Cooper had regained the European crown. Henry had returned to the well and found there was some water left – but not a lot! He'd boxed well, totally controlling the fight, but against a very crude and inexperienced opponent. To those who were prepared to look dispassionately at this performance, and of the one against Bodell in his last fight, it was obvious his best days were long gone. Even so, in the immediate aftermath of the contest, Wicks told the press Cooper had three more fights left, with two scheduled for South Africa early in 1971.

What of Urtain? The brave Basque would fight on for almost another seven years, participating in thirty four more contests, winning twenty one, losing nine and drawing the remainder. He'd knock out Jack Bodell to regain his European title, knock out Richard Dunn, draw with world title challenger, Jose Roman, and in 1977, in his last fight, he'd once again challenge, unsuccessfully, for the European crown. Maybe he was a better fighter than he was given credit for?

Jim Wicks was now making it clear he wanted Cooper to fight Joe Bugner next, and it's likely the idea of fighting in South Africa was simply a ruse to get Bugner into the ring. The big Hungarian was beginning to be talked up as a future world tile challenger, and he certainly looked the part. Many believed, however, that his management team were being over cautious in his development. When his team were approached about a challenge to Cooper for his three titles they were advised that Bugner needed another five or six fights before he'd be ready.

Yet another successful year ended on several high notes. At the beginning of December the Daily Express awarded Henry their Sportsman of the Year award and two weeks later he became the first person to win the hugely popular BBC Sports Personality of the Year award for a second time.

There was some confusion when a national newspaper reported that Henry had until the end of January to defend his European title against Jurgen Blin, but those rumours were quashed by the Boxing Board. Wicks was still insisting he was taking Cooper to South Africa in March for two contests, but admitted that if a promoter could arrange for him to defend his three titles, paying the proper purse of course, alternative arrangements could be made. In later years Henry would admit they'd decided his next fight would be his last, and if the three titles were to be on the line, the only suitable opponent, in terms of inflating the cash available, was Joe Bugner.

Wicks and Cooper were always totally honest with each other. Several journalists from that era have confirmed that Wicks looked after Cooper 'like a son', and there was no way he'd allow him to be hurt or humiliated. Cooper had begun to realise that the usual aches and strains were taking longer than expected to disappear. He'd also gradually come to notice that his sparring partners were able to cope with his heavy punches. Previously they would give up after a couple of days, having taken severe punishment from Cooper's left hooks, as he reached peak fitness. Now they were lasting the full duration. During one such session Cooper and Wicks had a knowing 'look' at each other and they both knew the time had come to bring the curtain down. Both of them would have been determined that the last fight should pay handsomely, and end on a winning note, retiring as undefeated champion.

In January 1971 the boxing world was alive with the news that Joe Frazier, now recognised universally as the champion, would fight the returning Muhammad Ali. Interestingly, and much to the credit of Cooper's advancing years, he was still rated in the world's top ten with Bodell and Bugner just below him. Cooper's life outside the ring was becoming increasingly congested with numerous engagements on radio and television. At that moment in time he was probably the most popular sportsman in Britain, and as such, was being continually invited to events, very few of which he ever refused.

Although Wicks was trying desperately to get the 'final' fight organised, a major stumbling block was the tax situation. It appeared that a contest prior to the end of the tax year would result in almost the entire purse being paid to the Inland Revenue. Nevertheless, Bugner's win over Carl Gizzi on 19 January seemed to have removed the final hurdle, and Harry Levene announced the fight would take place on 16 March at Wembley. Early reports indicated Cooper would receive in the region of £45,000 (£630,000) to Bugner's £15,000. Simultaneously the owner of Viewsport, Jarvis Astaire, offered Levene £50,000 for the rights to screen the contest live at cinemas throughout the country. Quite how Wicks managed the tax issue is unknown.

Levene and Astaire must've had some sleepless nights soon after, when they realised Bugner had yet another fight arranged in the intervening period at the York Hall in London against tough Canadian, Bill Drover. The bout was watched on TV by an estimated 9 million viewers who listened to Cooper assessing the fight between rounds. Referee Harry Gibbs scored the fight even, each man winning four rounds with the other two drawn. Thankfully Bugner emerged unscathed.

The boxing industry were waking up to the realisation that technology was the catalyst for huge sums to be earned by all those involved. With the use of satellites, live pictures could be broadcast all over the world and of course the television companies could attract significant revenues from advertisers. Heavyweight boxing was still the showpiece of the game and the forthcoming Frazier v Ali fight in New York was set to raise huge amounts of money. Those with a vested interest in British boxing knew that a capable heavyweight had the potential to break all financial records. This is where Joe Bugner's future came into sharp focus.

The naturalised Hungarian exile had everything. He was 6' 4", weighed in at fifteen and a half stones, blond, handsome, with a body like a Greek sculpture. He looked the part. However, there were many who also thought he fought like a great lump of Greek marble! That was partly why Cooper was a 3-1 on favourite. The problem was that this young man, who was reckoned to be the biggest heavyweight at the top level in world boxing at the time, didn't seem to have the aggression necessary to excite the public. He fought cautiously, and didn't seem to have a natural 'fighting' instinct. His Scottish manager Andy Smith would defend him from these accusations telling anyone who'd listen that he was being brought along carefully, learning as he went, but after thirty four fights in three years many felt he was now more than ready to throw caution to the wind.

From those fights Bugner had won thirty one, drawn two and lost only one – his first fight, when he was knocked out within three rounds. Perhaps anyone would've been cautious after such a start? There were a good list of 'names' on his winning record including Johnny Prescott, Manuel Ramos, Ray Patterson, Brian London, Chuck Wepner and Carl Gizzi. Significantly, for such a big man, only two of his wins had come by way of a clean knockout. The remainder were either a result of the referee stopping the fight because the opponents were being overwhelmed, or points decisions. Much of the criticism libelled at Bugner was unfair, when he fought Cooper he'd just turned twenty one, only a 'boy' compared to Henry. He'd done everything asked of him by his manager, and no matter what the critics said he was unbeaten in his last thirty three fights.

Boxing was taking centre stage in the sporting world at the beginning of March. Across the Atlantic Muhammad Ali was attempting to win back his world title in a fight billed as the 'Fight of the Century'. In many people's eyes Ali was still the champion given that he'd never lost his title in the ring. Moreover his legendary status meant that the casual fan viewed him as being simply invincible. At the same time the general public were becoming excited at the prospect, around a week later, of seeing Britain's own 'favourite son' defending his three titles against the new rising star of the heavyweight division.

Bugner prepared as normal at a former army barracks in St. Ives, twelve miles outside Cambridge. He was using Carl Gizzi and Bunny Johnson as sparring partners, who'd been instructed by Andy Smith to emulate Cooper's style. During the build up to the fight the BBC Sportsnight programme invited six former heavyweight stars to give their predictions. Erskine, Richardson, London, Walker and Jack Gardner all strongly favoured a Cooper victory, while Tommy Farr edged towards Bugner.

Cooper ,too, was preparing with his usual thoroughness. The team was based at the Clive Hotel in Hampstead while training at the Boxing Board's own gym next to the Noble Art pub on Haverstock Hill. Wicks, like Andy Smith, tried to get sparring partners who could copy the style of his opponent. Brought in were 6' 5" Welsh heavyweight Del Phillips and West Indian, Phil Dubisson, but finding other boxers as tall as Bugner wasn't easy.

The full build up in the media really only began once the 'Fight of the Century' reached a conclusion with Frazier smashing Ali onto his back in the last round before being awarded a clear points victory. To the dedicated boxing fan the result had been predictable, but the general public were shocked. They couldn't believe 'the Greatest' had been beaten so comprehensively.

As the momentum built towards Britain's own showdown, the national press came out in favour of a Cooper win. This was reflected in the bookmaker's odds for the fight. However the Boxing News produced an in-depth analysis, coming down on the side of a narrow Bugner victory. Their theory was that Henry's vaunted left hook was now not as potent, and if the younger challenger could survive the early rounds, he'd take the verdict. Correspondents Riley and Houston both went for Bugner, while Ron Olver favoured Cooper. In a further poll of managers Tommy Gilmour and Arthur Boggis supported Cooper while Tommy Miller, George Biddles and Bobby Neill plumped for Bugner. Boxers Jack Bodell, Mark Rowe and Pat McCormack sided with Cooper while Ken Buchanan believed Bugner could do it.

107

It had been over ten years since anyone in 'the game' seriously considered another British heavyweight could pose a threat to Henry's dominance.

Cooper's popularity had a definite influence on the public's perception on how the fight would progress. It wasn't a case that Bugner was disliked, it was just that Henry had become a British icon, and people don't like to see an icon put down. It was later revealed that on the morning of the fight the large bookmakers were becoming concerned at the money being poured on to a Bugner victory. His odds had dropped from 3-1 to 6-4, in other wards they'd halved. When these events happen there's always speculation that 'someone' has inside knowledge which would affect the outcome. Wicks was contacted by at least one leading bookmaker enquiring if Cooper was injured in some way, but that rumour was quickly dismissed. Nevertheless, the swing in the betting odds just prior to the fight continued to attract sinister speculation long after the contest ended.

For decades after the fight, discussions centred not on the content of the fight, nor did they focus on the performance of either man. The central figure turned out to be the referee, Harry Gibbs.

There have never been clear guidelines on how a professional referee, or judge, should score a fight. It's not simply a matter of toting up clean punches landed and awarding each round to whoever lands the most. Mostly it's about the experienced official's impression of who deserves to win a round, and this may bring in factors such as 'ring dominance', 'power' punches landed, defensive skills and willingness to attack. Therefore, in a close contest, opinions can differ widely, even amongst referees and/or judges. For the Cooper v Bugner fight, Gibbs was the sole arbiter.

In 1981 Harry Gibbs discussed his officiating of the bout in his autobiography, and this included a copy of his scorecard. The film of the entire fight is widely available including Harry Carpenter's rather biased commentary, allowing a modern day review of the fight alongside Gibbs's scorecard. The following analysis of the fight, while based solely on opinion, might provide a sense of completeness to the Cooper boxing story.

Round 1: Gibbs gave the round to Bugner. The film of the fight though, suggests it would be virtually impossible for the unbiased observer to score the round for the challenger. It was admittedly very close, but if a decision had to be made, it surely should have been given to Cooper.

Round 2: Gibbs gave the round to Bugner. This was indeed a clear winning round for Bugner who landed good double jabs with very little coming back in response from Cooper.

Round 3: Gibbs gave the round to Cooper. Cooper probably deserved the vote from Gibbs due to his attacks, but it was close again. Henry was cut on the left eyebrow.

Round 4: Gibbs gave the round to Bugner. Bugner landed several sharp left hooks and was also successful with left and right hands to the body on the inside.

Round 5: Gibbs gave the round to Cooper. Long range body punches from Cooper plus his attacking may have edged it, but it was very tight. Bugner could not have won it, but it might have justifiably been scored even. Harry Carpenter suggested it was the most clear round of the fight!

Round 6: Gibbs gave the round to Bugner. Cooper appeared to control the first half of the round before Bugner came back strongly. Scoring the round would be down to preference. The logical option was to score it even.

Round 7: Gibbs marked this as an even round, but it seemed a good clear winning round for Bugner. Hardly any offensive blows coming from Cooper, and Bugner scored regularly with double jabs. Cooper cut under the right eye.

Round 8: Gibbs again marked this round as a draw. This was probably the correct scoring. It was an unremarkable round with the only memorable blow being landed by Cooper's right hand. Both men looked to be tiring.

Round 9: Gibbs gave this to Bugner. There was more action in this round. Both men seemed determined to get the upper hand and stronger punches were landing. Another very close round but in the last minute Bugner landed more often and seemed to clinch it.

Round 10: Gibbs again made this a drawn round. Cooper clearly won this using any interpretation of scoring a fight. Two big left hooks landed and much more aggression from the champion.

With two thirds of the fight over Gibbs had scored five rounds to Bugner, two to Cooper and three even. An alternative view might suggest that the contest was extremely close at four rounds to each and two drawn. Gibbs believed that Cooper had looked very lethargic and didn't really come into the fight until about the ninth round. A rather unusual statement given that he gave that particular round to Bugner?

Peter Wilson, who at the time was a very experienced and highly respected, specialist, boxing correspondent for the Daily Mirror had given Cooper six rounds, Bugner three, with one even.

Round 11: Gibbs scored this round even. During the fight commentary Harry Carpenter believed Cooper won the round but it's difficult to see it that way. It was extremely close and virtually impossible to award it to either boxer.

Round 12: Gibbs gave the round to Cooper. This was a very tough round for both boxers but towards the end of the session Bugner might just have edged it due to his clean jabs.

Round 13: Gibbs awarded the round to Cooper and he couldn't have done otherwise. This was the most dominant round of the fight for the champion. He landed cleanly, and often, with Bugner very much on the receiving end of the barrage.

Round 14: Gibbs gave another round to Cooper. Henry continued where he left off in the previous round. Coming forward and landing clean jabs with very little coming back in response.

Going into the last round on Gibbs's official scorecard the fight was drawn with both boxers having taken five rounds each with four even. On the other hand Cooper may well have been one round in front, by six rounds to five and three drawn. Peter Wilson's view from his ringside seat was that Bugner hadn't won a round from the eleventh to the fourteenth!

Round 15: Gibbs gave it to Bugner. This was an accurate reflection of the round, Bugner gave it everything he had and Cooper had difficulty matching him.

When Gibbs raised Bugner's hand the crowd erupted in a chorus of boos. Harry Carpenter couldn't believe it, sounding disgusted at the verdict. Peter Wilson, in his report for the Daily Mirror, couldn't give Bugner more than four rounds. The furore over the decision would continue for decades.

There has been so much speculation about the events surrounding the fight, some of it even involving litigation. Did the swing in the betting odds signal that something untoward had taken place? There were several in the Cooper camp who felt that Bugner got the decision because the officials knew this was Henry's last fight, and if he'd retired as the champion the title picture would have been unsettled for months if not years to come. The unproven rumour was that if the fight was close Gibbs would give the decision to the younger man.

Henry Cooper: Cut Eyes and Left Hooks

Looking back in hindsight it's likely that most of the hysteria about the decision was down to pure nostalgia and sentimentality. Henry was such a popular individual, and as the champion, he was part of a long held misconception among the boxing world that a challenger had to win decisively to capture a title. In other words, in a very close fight, the champion should retain. This of course was nonsense.

Henry never really forgave Harry Gibbs, and Gibbs himself was very brittle with anyone who challenged his verdict. It does seem very likely that Gibbs was an honest referee who scored the fight as he saw it without any obvious outside interference. We must remember it was a very close battle, and regardless of who'd won, it didn't deserve such widespread outrage.

Nevertheless, there remains a possibility that Gibbs could subconsciously have caused the animosity heaped upon him by the unpopular outcome. Gibbs was a Londoner, coming from the same part of the capital as Cooper, but he was also a proud and independent man who didn't like his judgement or integrity to be challenged. There's every possibility that Gibbs, believing Cooper would either stop Bugner or have too much experience in the long run for his younger opponent, and in an effort to show how unbiased he was towards his fellow Londoner, began to score some of the early, close rounds, to Bugner, in the expectation that it wouldn't make any difference at the end of the day. The first and sixth rounds could be examples of this theory.

Only when Gibbs began to realise the fight would likely travel the full distance did he perhaps begin to realise his misjudgement. A possible example of Gibbs's attempt to redress the balance might be found in the scoring of the twelfth round which he gave to Cooper. That session could easily be viewed by some observers as one which should have been given to Bugner. Gibbs said himself in his autobiography that when he was totting up the scores prior to the last round starting, the thought passed through his mind, "Thank God Cooper's an old pro, surely he must have saved something for the last round." That statement alone tends to support this argument.

Henry had lost his final fight and three titles, to the first of the third generation of British heavyweights he had to contend with over his seventeen years in the game, and, sadly, with his former trainer, Danny Holland, in the opposite corner tending to any cuts sustained by Bugner.

111

The new triple champion lost all his hard earned titles five months later to Jack Bodell and wouldn't have them back in his grasp once more until he beat Richard Dunn in October 1976. In between times he performed creditably to lose on points to both Ali and Frazier before trying unsuccessfully for the world title against Ali again, losing a wide decision over fifteen rounds. Bugner eventually emigrated to Australia and had his last contest in June 1999 an incredible twenty eight years after facing Cooper. Sadly, Bugner never became a favourite with the British public. Many put this down to his unpopular win over Henry but in reality his relatively cautious approach to contests seemed to prevent him opening up and going for the impressive stoppage victory so often demanded from the big men of the sport. The hardcore boxing fan didn't appreciate his performances.

Conclusion

WHEN AN ERA COMES TO ITS END, THE BOXING WORLD, LIKE LIFE IN general, moves on. The promoters, managers, journalists and all the rest, had to look to the future, a heavyweight future, without Henry Cooper. Henry's departure left a huge gap in that division, which perhaps was not really filled until the arrival of the ever popular Frank Bruno some fifteen years later. Cooper's future outside the ring, however, was assured. Not only had he made a tidy sum from his boxing career but the ground work had already begun on his new, and lucrative role, as a media celebrity.

It's difficult to look back on his career without the distraction of wearing 'rose tinted spectacles'. Henry was everyone's hero. His face was instantly recognisable well before the days of mass communication. Even people who had no interest in boxing knew he'd knocked down Cassius Clay. They knew he'd twice won the BBC Sports Personality of the Year award and saw him regularly advertising on the 'telly'. If we ignore for a moment his endearing character, and simply analyse his performances in the ring we can come closer to answering the question often posed, then and now – "how good a boxer was Cooper?"

The bold statistics show that from fifty five contests, he won forty, lost fourteen and drew once. Not a bad record, but not outstanding, although the quality of his opposition has to be taken into account. He'd four fights with boxers who at one time or another held the world title. He'd a further eight fights with boxers who'd challenged for the world title and he'd an additional six fights against men who'd held the European title.

From around October 1958 until he retired some twelve years later Cooper was reckoned by most sources to have been within the world's top ten heavyweights. So he was certainly a world class boxer, but, admittedly, fell short of being part of the elite. The first boxer he fought who became a world champion was Ingemar

Johansson. The Swede's big right hand punch separated Henry from his consciousness within five rounds and they never boxed again. Some six years later he took on Cassius Clay, a rising star at the time. In that fight he landed his most famous punch to flatten the Kentuckian and if it'd landed thirty seconds earlier world boxing history would have been re-written. As it was, Cooper was halted in the very next round with a badly gashed eyebrow.

In 1966 Cooper made his only challenge for the world title against the same man, now known as Mohammed Ali. Henry once again gave a good account of himself but the bout ended in the sixth round with his eye bleeding like a waterfall. Five months later in an attempt to put himself back into world title contention he took on the former champion, Floyd Patterson, and similar to his bout with Johansson, it ended with Henry concussed. These contests proved that Cooper did not reach the very top level in world terms.

In Cooper's eight fights with boxers who'd challenged for world honours he was more successful. In his three fights with Brian London, who'd fought both Patterson and Ali, Cooper won them all. In two fights with Zora Folley, who would face Ali, Henry won and lost, and in September 1960 he beat Roy Harris who'd fought Patterson. He also stopped Karl Mildenberger who lost to Ali, and was beaten by Joe Bugner, who would also lose to the 'Greatest'.

Dick Richardson was a former European champion, and Cooper stopped the big Welshman on the two occasions they fought. Jack Bodell would go on to win the European title and Henry beat him twice. Henry beat Urtain, and his draw with Heinz Neuhaus, another former European champion, shouldn't be forgotten. For virtually his entire seventeen year career Cooper was at the very peak of heavyweight boxing in Europe.

Except for an 'administrative' blip in 1969, Cooper held the British title for twelve years, winning three Lonsdale belts in the process. Once he was able to overcome the skilful Joe Erskine, until the disputed defeat to Bugner, there was no one in Britain who seriously challenged his supremacy.

Arguably there are two fights which might be used to define Cooper's status as a heavyweight during the seventeen years of his career, each separated by a period of just under seven years. The first was in December 1961 when he fought the highly ranked Zora Folley for the second time. Henry had been accelerated into the top three contenders for the world title following his victory over Folley three years earlier. It would later transpire that Folley, reluctantly, conceded that when they fought the first time he didn't have sufficient time to prepare, and his extra weight at the time of the fight would tend to support his assertion.

In 1961 Folley was still one of the best heavyweights in the world, and Henry had just secured his first Lonsdale belt. At twenty seven years of age Cooper could well have been at his absolute peak when the fight took place. For the short time the fight lasted it became obvious that Folley had learned a great deal from their first fight. The American knew exactly how to counteract Henry's principal weapon, the left jab. Very early in the fight Folley stood his ground and swung over a big right hand punch, which although it didn't land cleanly, made Cooper wary. In the second round Cooper was still throwing the left jab but with much less conviction, when Folley's big punch landed with full force and the fight was over. It must have been clear to Jim Wicks, and those in the London boxing community who were not influenced by Henry's popularity, that it was unlikely he would be able to fulfil his world championship ambitions.

On a more positive note, the second defining fight, in September 1968, against Karl Mildenberger established Cooper as the top European heavyweight of his generation. Coming into the fight Henry hadn't fought for ten months, and at thirty four years of age his injuries were beginning to catch up with him. His left hand, left elbow and troublesome knees were restricting his preparations. His German opponent held the European crown and had no intention of giving it up. It'd only been a few months since he'd taken Ali into the twelfth round in a world title challenge.

On that night at Wembley Cooper gave perhaps his best ever performance. From the first bell he totally dominated proceedings with his left hand leaving Mildenberger confused and ineffectual. The champion was well on the way to a punishing defeat when he was disqualified in the eighth round for deliberately butting Cooper. Even in his advancing years, Henry again demonstrated he was simply too good for the European heavyweights of the time.

There is no point in comparing Henry to British heavyweights from different eras. In modern times, with improved nutrition and better health provisions heavyweight boxers are much bigger and heavier. Conversely, going back in history, heavyweight boxers were generally smaller, used different boxing gloves and had very basic training methods. To try to analyse how a boxer from one era would have fared against a boxer from a different age, is equivalent to comparing apples with pears. What we can say about Cooper is that for most of his career he was undoubtedly the best heavyweight in Britain. For a slightly shorter period, since the retirement of Johansson in fact, he was the best heavyweight in Europe and simultaneously was within the top ten best heavyweights in the world. I believe Henry himself would be satisfied with this summation.

Fight Record

Date	Opponent	Venue	Weight	Result
14.09.54	Harry Painter	Harringay	13st 6lb	W ko R1
19.10.54	Dinny Powell	Harringay	13st 7lb	W rsf R4
23.11.54	Eddie Keith	Manor Place	13st 9lb	W rsf R1
7.12.54	Denny Ball	Harringay	13st 7lb	W ko R3
27.01.55	Colin Strauch	Albert Hall	13st 7lb	W rsf R1
08.02.55	Cliff Purnell	Harringay	13st 11lb	W pts 6 Rds
08.03.55	Hugh Ferns	Earls Court	13st 9lb	W dis R2
29.03.55	Joe Crickmar	Empress Hall	13st 11lb	W rtd R5
18.04.55	Joe Bygraves	Manor Place	13st 10lb	W pts 8Rds
26.04.55	Uber Bacilieri	Harringay	13st 8lb	L cuts R2
06.06.55	Ron Harman	Nottingham	13st 4lb	W rsf R7
13.09 55	Uber Bacilieri	White City	13st 5lb	W ko R7
15.11.55	Joe Erskine	Harringay	13st 7lb	L pts 10 Rds
28.02.56	Maurice Mols	Albert Hall	14st	W rsf R4
01.05.56	Brian London	Empress Hall	13st 9lb	W rsf R1
26.06.56	Giannino Luise	Wembley	13st 11lb	W rsf R7
07.09.56	Peter Bates	Manchester	13st 9lb	L cuts Rtd R5
19.02 57	Joe Bygraves	Earls Court	14st	L ko R9
British Empire Title				
19.05.57	Ingemar Johansson	Stockholm	13st 12lb	L ko R5
European Title				
17.09.57	Joe Erskine	Harringay	13st 8lb	L pts 15 Rds
British Title				
16.11.57	Hans Kalbfell	Dortmund	no weight	W pts 10 Rds
11.01.58	Heinz Neuhaus	Dortmund	13st 11lb	D 10 Rds

Jim Kirkwood

Date	Opponent	Venue	Weight	Result
19.04.58	Erich Schoeppner	Frankfurt	no weight	L disq R6
03.09.58	Dick Richardson	Porthcawl	13st 6lb	W rsf R5
14.10.58	Zora Folley	Wembley	13st 7lb	W pts 10 Rds
12.01.59	Brian London	Earls Court	13st 11lb	W pts 15 Rds
British and Empire Titles				
26.08.59	Gawie de Klerk	Porthcawl	13st 3lb	W rsf R5
Empire Title				
17.11.59	Joe Erskine	Earls Court	13st 7lb	W rsf R12
British and Empire Titles				
13.09.60	Roy Harris	Wembley	13st 3lb	W pts 10 Rds
06.12.60	Alex Miteff	Wembley	13st 8lb	W pts 10 Rds
21.03.61	Joe Erskine	Wembley	13st 6lb	W rtd R5
British and Empire Titles				
05.12.61	Zora Folley	Wembley	13st 7lb	L ko R2
23.01.62	Tony Hughes	Wembley	13st 9lb	W rtd R5
26.02.62	Wayne Bethea	Manchester	13st 7lb	W pts R10
02.04.62	Joe Erskine	Nottingham	13st 10lb	W rsf R9
British and Empire Titles				
26.03.63	Dick Richardson	Wembley	13st 6lb	W ko R5
British and Empire Titles				
18.06.63	Cassius Clay	Wembley	13st 4lb	L rsf R5
24.02.64	Brian London	Manchester	13st 7lb	W pts 15 Rds
British, Empire and European Titles				
16.11.64	Roger Rischer	Albert Hall	13st 7lb	L pts 10 Rds
12.01.65	Dick Wipperman	Albert Hall	13st 8lb	W rsf R5
20.04.65	Chip Johnson	Wolverhampton	13st 11lb	W ko R1
15.06.65	Johnny Prescott	Birmingham	13st 5lb	W rtd R10
British and Empire Titles				
19.10.65	Amos Johnson	Wembley	13st 8lb	L pts 10 Rds
25.01.66	Hubert Hilton	Olympia	13st 10lb	W rsf R2
16.02.66	Jefferson Davis	Wolverhampton	13st 9lb	W ko R1
21.05.66	Muhammad Ali	Highbury	13st 6lb	L rsf R6

Henry Cooper: Cut Eyes and Left Hooks

Date	Opponent	Venue	Weight	Result
World Title				
20.09.66	Floyd Patterson	Wembley	13st 10lb	L ko R4
17.04.67	Boston Jacobs	Leicester	13st 12lb	W pts 10 Rds
13.06.67	Jack Bodell	Wolverhampton	13st 7lb	W rsf R2
British and Empire Titles				
07.11.67	Billy Walker	Wembley	13st 6lb	W rsf R6
British and Empire Titles				
18.09.68	Karl Mildenberger	Wembley	13st 5lb	W disq R8
European Title				
13.03.69	Piero Tomasoni	Rome	13st 6lb	W ko R5
European Title				
24.03.70	Jack Bodell	Wembley	14st 3lb	W pts 15 Rds
British and Commonwealth Titles				
10.11.70	Jose Urtain	Wembley	13st 8lb	W rsf R9
European Title				
16.03.71	Joe Bugner	Wembley	13st 7lb	L pts 15 Rds
British, European and Commonwealth Titles				